Foreword

The integrated waste management option
Zero Waste
by Stephen Tindale, Greenpeace Executive Director

I	**Waste and the Environment**	5
II	**Zero Waste**	18
III	**The growth of recycling**	31
IV	**The Road to Zero Waste**	47
V	**The Green Materials Revolution**	69
VI	**The Transition to Zero Waste**	82
VII	**Re-orienting UK waste**	91
VIII	**The integrated option**	109
IX	**A Zero Waste Policy for Britain**	129
X	**Beyond Recycling**	167
	Conclusion	187
	Endnotes	198

Foreword

Stephen Tindale, Greenpeace Executive Director

The issue of waste has become a political hot potato. Central government wants 'sustainable waste management' but passes the buck to local authorities. Local authorities decry the lack of funds from central government to enable anything but the cheapest option and reproach householders for failing to participate in reduction and recycling schemes. And the public opposes waste disposal facilities – both incinerators and landfill – with a vehemence they normally reserve for nuclear waste dumps.

A new awareness that our society faces a waste crisis has moved waste management from a marginal issue to one at the centre of political debate. Some are stricken with panic at the prospect of overhauling the waste system, but at the same time a new, more positive attitude is emerging. There is now a far greater willingness to see waste as an opportunity and to see the solutions as part of a wider agenda stretching from climate change through resource management to urban regeneration.

As Robin Murray eloquently explains in this book, 'from the perspective of pollution, the problem is a question of what waste is. From the perspective of resource productivity, it is a question of what waste could be. As a pollutant, waste demands controls. As an embodiment of accumulated energy and materials it invites an alternative. The one is a constraint to an old way of doing things. The other opens up a path to the new.'

What is emerging is a polarisation of approaches to waste. One clings desperately to the old way of doing things, the other embraces the new and drives further change. This book details the failings of the old, business-as-usual option, that has been dressed up in the new clothes of 'integrated waste management'. It then outlines a new approach, a Zero Waste policy, that promises to transform attitudes to waste, the organisational forms used to manage it and, crucially, the systems that produce it. Perhaps most importantly it outlines practical policy measures necessary to achieve this.

The integrated waste management option

The race is now on to draw up 'sustainable' waste strategies. But the failure of central government, and most waste disposal authorities, to make any serious progress with the 'reduce, reuse, recycle' paradigm during the last decade, has led to the emergence of a national policy in the UK that encourages strategies that are anything but sustainable.

This policy, and the local strategies based on it, are referred to as 'integrated waste management'. Based on a simple forecasting model that predicts a maximum recycling level of around 40% and a continued increase in municipal waste generation, the 'integrated option' relies on incinerators, or other forms of thermal treatment, to deal with the large predicted residual waste stream.

Integrated waste management policies nominally give primacy to waste minimisation, recycling and composting, but inevitably solve the 'disposal problem' through incinerator-reliant packages. The incinerator element commits us to a future in which increasing levels of pollutants such as dioxin, a known carcinogen, will be generated and dispersed to air and land. Meanwhile, much recyclable material will be lost to disposal along with most of the energy contained within it, and opportunities for jobs and community participation will likewise be bypassed.

Incinerators lock us into an eternal present of waste generation and disposal. The capital investment they embody and their relentless hunger for feedstock places a very real cap on minimisation, reuse and recycling of waste for at least a generation. They provide an easy option for waste that stifles innovation, imagination and incentives. They effectively kill off the possibility of transforming waste management from its current obsession with cheap disposal to the genuinely worthwhile goal of high added-value resource utilisation.

Thus integrated waste management precludes the radical new approach to waste that is urgently needed. Fortunately there is a way out of this cul-de-sac.

Zero Waste

The first and most obvious question from the casual observer confronted by the concept of 'Zero Waste' is, 'Can it be achieved?'.

The term Zero Waste has its origins in the highly successful Japanese industrial concept of total quality management (TQM). It is influenced by ideas such as 'zero defects', the extraordinarily successful approach whereby producers like Toshiba have achieved results as low as one defect per million. Transferred to the arena of municipal waste, Zero Waste forces attention onto the whole lifecycle of products.

Zero Waste encompasses producer responsibility, ecodesign, waste reduction, reuse and recycling, all within a single framework. It breaks away from the inflexibility of incinerator-centred systems and offers a new policy framework capable of transforming current linear production and disposal processes into 'smart' systems that utilise the resources in municipal waste and generate jobs and wealth for local economies.

The right question to ask, then, is not (yet) whether Zero Waste can be achieved, but how can it be used as a policy driver, to free us from the disposal cul-de-sac and break through the currently perceived limits to minimisation and recycling?

Robin Murray is one of the world's leading thinkers on waste issues. In this book he describes a system of waste management that addresses all the environmental problems associated with conventional waste disposal and outlines the political, financial and organisational changes necessary to implement this system.

The Zero Waste policy Murray describes could move Britain to the forefront of modern 'smart' waste management. As such, it provides a beacon for politicians wishing to move the UK from the dark ages of waste disposal to a new era of Zero Waste.

I Waste and the Environment

Waste policy has become one of the most keenly contested areas of environmental politics. At a local level in the UK and abroad, the siting of landfills and incinerators has provoked degrees of civil opposition matched only by proposals for new roads and nuclear power plants. Nationally and internationally, there has been hand-to-hand fighting in the institutions of governance over clauses, targets and definitions of the strategies and regulative regimes that are shaping a new era for waste management.

For those professionally involved in the waste industry in Britain, it is as though a searchlight has suddenly been shone on an activity that for a hundred years was conducted in obscurity. Throughout the twentieth century, waste was the terminus of industrial production. Like night cleaners, the waste industry had the task of removing the debris from the main stage of daily activity. Some of the debris had value and was recycled. Most was deposited in former mines, gravel pits and quarries or, via incinerators, was 'landfilled in the air'. The principle was to keep it out of sight. Whereas consumer industries seek publicity, this post-consumer industry prided itself on its invisibility.

In the past twenty years, this situation has changed dramatically. Waste has moved from the margins to the political mainstream. The prime mover has been a new awareness of the pollution caused by the disposal of waste. This has been, and still is, the entry point for communities and governments becoming involved in what has hitherto been an untouchable issue. But there is now also a recognition of the significance of waste for two other major environmental issues – climate change and resource depletion. For policy makers the question of what to do about the targets reached at the Kyoto summit on climate change is also a question of what to do about waste. Similarly, issues of the world's forest cover, of mining degradation and soil loss cast a new perspective on old newspapers and discarded tin cans.

From the perspective of pollution, the problem is a question of what waste is. From the perspective of resource productivity, it is a question of what waste could become. As a pollutant, waste demands controls. As an embodiment of accumulated energy and materials it invites an alternative. The one is a constraint to an old way of doing things. The other opens up a path to the new. Any discussion of waste policy, of local waste plans and of their economic consequences must start from these three issues: pollution, climate change and resource depletion.

Pollution control

The acknowledgement of the significance of waste for the environment is comparatively recent. It was only in the 1970s that the poisoning of watercourses by the leachate from landfills became generally recognised, together with the risk of explosion and the toxic effects of air particles on those living in the neighbourhood of landfills. A recent European survey, based on Swedish evidence, has suggested that landfills are a significant source of the highly toxic carcinogen, dioxins, principally through air dispersion and the impact of landfill fires. A range of epidemiological studies found elevated rates of cancer, birth defects, low birth weights and small size of children in households living close to landfills.[1]

In the UK, the dangers associated with landfills were reinforced by the publication, in August 2001, of a study on the health effects of living near landfills. Focussing on 9,565 landfills in the UK, the study found that the risk of birth defects increased by 1% for those living within 2km of a landfill (and by 7% for those near special waste sites). For neural tube defects like spina bifida, the increase was 5%, for genital defects it was 7% and for abdominal defects 8%. Since 80% of the UK population lives within 2km of a landfill site, this study has posted a general health warning on Britain's predominant means of disposal.[2]

In addition, landfill was early identified as a major source of methane, one of the principal greenhouse gases, that contributes 20% of global warming. In the UK, landfills account for more than a quarter of all methane produced. For the EU as a whole, the figure in 1999 was 32%.[3] The methane given off in the process of decomposition of organic waste in landfills carries with it the local dangers of contamination and explosion in addition to its contribution to climate change. As these effects have become known, there has been increased resistance to the opening of new landfills throughout the developed world. Planners have often referred to this as self-interested 'nimbyism'[4], but the resistance has developed into a much wider critique of waste and the hazards associated with it.[5]

It was also discovered that incinerators, the main traditional disposal alternative to landfills, and widely adopted in countries where landfilling was difficult (such as Japan, Switzerland, Holland and Scandinavia) have been a major source of pollution. In their case, the problem has not been with organic waste but with materials which give off toxic emissions when burnt. Early tracking of the source of dioxins and furans identified incinerators as the prime source and even in the mid-1990s, when other sources were uncovered, municipal incinerators still accounted for over a third of all estimated emissions. They were also important sources of the release of volatile metals such as mercury, cadmium and lead.[6]

The health impacts of incinerator pollution on air, water, and land (through the landfilling or spreading of toxic ash) have been the subject of an intense and expanding scientific debate.[7] Few now dispute the extreme toxicity of many of the substances produced by incinerators. In spite of repeated plant upgrades and the introduction of new flue gas treatment technologies, municipal incinerators and other forms of 'thermal waste treatment' such as pyrolysis and gasification remain at core dirty technologies for four reasons:

(i) if flue gas emissions are reduced through improved scrubbing and cleaning, this does not destroy the toxic residues but transfers them to the ash, and creates the problem of the safe disposal of toxic ash and of polluted wastewater;[8]

(ii) municipal incinerators and thermal treatment plants are not dealing with streams of a single material with a standard calorific value. There are constant changes in the composition of the waste, in its calorific values and its moisture content. This means that there are difficulties in operating these plants at the consistent combustion conditions necessary to minimise the toxicity of emissions;

(iii) the inclusion of volatile substances and fluctuating highly combustible materials is one of the reasons for the regular fires, process upsets (and even explosions) that characterise incineration, and which in turn lead to large increases in toxic emissions;[9]

(iv) it is difficult to control the illicit introduction of toxic waste into incinerators, or of materials such as PVC, which can be major sources of dioxin when burnt.

For all these reasons there has been a continuing gap between the government's view of the effectiveness of incinerator pollution control via regulation and local experience of the impact of incinerators. It is a gap between ideal and 'actually existing' incineration. One measure of the gap is the data on regulatory 'exceedances' by incinerators.[10] Another is the epidemiological and contamination evidence of those who live near them. A third is the evidence on the hazardous conditions faced by those working in incineration plants. The gap defines an increasingly intense space of environmental politics, one that centres on information, and is engaged principally at the level of local and regional policy, planning inquiries and elections.[11]

Landfills and incinerators have highlighted the problems of the toxicity of waste and how it has traditionally been managed. In part the new awareness can be seen as an aspect of the knowledge revolution, a result of improved measurement technology which has brought to light many longstanding problems which previously went unmeasured. But in part it is a response to the growing toxicity of modern materials themselves.

In landfills the decomposition of waste leads to emissions from many of the 100,000 chemicals now in use in modern production, while the acidifying process of biological degradation leaches out dangerous substances. With incineration, a core problem has been with those materials known to be particularly toxic when burnt (such as chlorine-based products, batteries and brominated flame-retardants). In each case the dangers associated with particular hazardous materials are compounded when their disposal is part of a general waste stream.

As these effects have been recognised, the response has been increased regulations and improved technology. Modern landfills are required to be lined, and to treat the leachate and burn the gases emitted from the sites. Incinerators in Europe have had to be upgraded with new flue gas treatment technologies, which have cut toxic emissions to air. In this, the policies to control pollution from waste are part (if a later part) of the wider regulatory history of pollution abatement which characterised environmental policy in the last quarter of the twentieth century.

Yet in the case of waste, more stringent regulations have far from solved the problems. A large number of current (and past) landfill sites lack leachate and gas treatment. Those that have installed them have not been able to eliminate toxic emissions to air and water.[12] The improved flue gas cleaning at incinerators has reduced air emissions but not stopped them. There are still regular exceedances, and as we have seen there are still problems with the handling and disposal of the toxic ash. Incinerators remain generators of pollution which is dispersed widely (by design) via stack emissions, ash spreading, ash burial and water discharges.

There are no reliable, risk-free technologies for waste

disposal. The issue of toxicity is a shadow over the present management of waste that will not go away.

Climate change

If waste is a threat, it is now also seen as an opportunity – nowhere more so than in relation to climate change. At one level, it is a question of cutting emissions – of methane in the case of landfill or of carbon dioxide (CO_2) and oxides of nitrogen (NOx) in the case of incineration. Equally significant is the potential contribution of waste management in displacing other global warming activities and in acting as a carbon sink. In the words of the US Environmental Protection Agency (EPA) in 1998:

"Among the efforts to slow the potential for climate change are measures to reduce emissions of carbon dioxide from energy use, reduce methane emissions and change forestry practices to promote long-term storage of carbon in trees. Different management options for Municipal Solid Waste provide many opportunities to affect these same processes, directly or indirectly."[13]

Of these, the most significant is the opportunity to retain the energy embodied in waste products by reuse and recycling. One quarter of greenhouse gas (GHG) emissions stem from the life cycle of materials. Any substitution of the demand for primary materials by the reuse and recycling of secondary materials and discarded products stands to contribute significant savings in energy and the resulting emissions.[14]

One estimate of the savings has been made for the USA in an exhaustive study by the USEPA. In the USA, nearly half the municipal waste is accounted for by five materials – paper, steel, aluminium, glass and plastic. The virgin production of these materials consumes one third of all manufacturing industry's energy consumption. According to the USEPA study, recycling these materials rather than disposing of them by landfill or incineration would result in savings of 0.8 metric tonnes of carbon equivalent (MTCE) for every tonne of waste diverted, or 17 million MTCE for each 10% of municipal waste diverted from disposal.[15]

For the UK, the intensive diversion of waste from disposal has a similarly striking impact. One model that used the USEPA data on relative CO2 effects found that the reuse and recycling of 70% of the UK's municipal waste would lead to a saving of 14.8 million MTCE, which would have a similar impact to taking 5.4 million cars off the road.[16] If this was repeated for commercial and industrial waste, the total savings would amount to nearly a third of the reductions (over and above existing measures) that would be necessary for the UK to meet its target of 20% cuts in CO2 by 2010. This is one measure of the significance of waste diversion within the context of the Kyoto protocol.[17]

There are two other ways in which the form of waste management can reduce net CO2 emissions. The first is the impact of using composted biodegradable waste on land as a soil amendment and, in doing so, 'sequestering' carbon from its everyday cycle. Applying compost acts as a counterweight to the release of stored-up carbon in soils resulting from depletion induced by intensive agriculture. This is an area of increasing scientific interest in the context of agricultural and climatic sustainability. One estimate is that 20 billion tonnes a year of carbon are captured in the soil's organic matter, compared with 80 billion tonnes of anthropogenic carbon emitted to the atmosphere.[18] In Italy, Favoino cites evidence to suggest that an increase of 0.15% of organic carbon would lock the same amount of carbon into soil biomass as is released annually into the atmosphere by the use of fossil fuels in Italy.[19] The significance of composting for carbon sequestration in soils was recognised by the recent Bonn Conference on Climate Change and is becoming an increasing influence in EU policy.

The other potential impact of waste management on CO2 reduction is more controversial, based as it is on the production of power (and in some cases heat) from incinerators. The energy value of waste materials is 5% of primary energy consumption, using Western European data.[20] Until the publication of the USEPA results, it was commonly argued that burning the combustible elements of waste – particularly paper, plastic and wood – was environmentally more beneficial than recycling them, and there have even been attempts to suggest that the same holds for burning organic waste rather than composting it. From this perspective it is argued that waste should be reconceptualised as a renewable energy source, a form of bio-energy similar to coppice wood, with incineration a significant contributor to the shift from fossil fuel to renewable energy production.

There have been three main objections to this argument:

- plastics are derived from fossil fuel, and their combustion may well produce more CO_2 than the electricity sources they displace;

- the energy value of organic waste is low, at 4 megajoules (MJ) per kg.

- the increased demand for paper, even with 39% recycled input worldwide, is leading both to the destruction of original natural forests, particularly in the South and the former Soviet bloc, and to the growth of plantation forests. Leaving aside the implications of these trends for biodiversity, acidification, erosion and water quality, recycling paper rather than prematurely burning it would allow old growth forests currently due for felling, as in Finland, to remain standing (and thus to continue to act as a carbon sink) or would allow fully grown wood destined for pulp manufacture to be used directly as a biomass fuel, thus preserving the energy already embodied in waste paper.[21]

Since the USEPA results and parallel studies in the EU, there has been a shift in the argument – away from the environmental benefits of incineration over recycling, to the recovery of energy from residual waste that has no value as a recyclate. In parallel the research debate has moved from life cycle analyses of incineration and recycling to models showing the maximum practicable level of recycling, thus defining a boundary beyond which incineration no longer competes with recycling but produces net savings in CO_2. The issue of maximum recycling levels will be discussed more fully later. Here it is enough to note that there is agreement on the potential for recycling and composting to reduce fossil fuel energy production and emissions of CO_2.

Ecosystems and resource productivity

In the past five years a third argument for waste recycling has come to the fore – namely the impact that it can have on reducing the pressure of industrial growth on primary resources. An early version of the argument was framed in terms of the 'limits to growth' and the impossibility of generalising the current model of material intensive production to the developing world. The limits were described primarily in resource terms. Economists replied that the price mechanism plus new technology would deal with scarcities, citing evidence that material supplies have continually run ahead of demand and that primary product prices – far from rising – are now approaching a thirty-year low.

The modern version of the argument is wider and is posed in terms of ecological systems rather than particular resources as such. The stock of the 'natural capital' is being run down, depleting the life supporting services provided by natural systems. In the words of three articulate exponents of the case:

"It is not the supplies of oil or copper that are beginning to limit our development but life itself. Today our continuing progress is restricted not by the number of fishing boats but by the decreasing numbers of fish; not by the power of pumps but the depletion of aquifers; not by the number of chainsaws but by the disappearance of primary forests ... Humankind has inherited a 3.8 billion-year store of natural capital. At present rates of use and degradation, there will be little left by the end of the [21st] century."[22]

The destruction of natural systems such as fresh water and marine ecosystems, forest cover and soil nutrients is not adequately reflected in the price system, since they are either free (like access to common land), or subject to 'founders rent' – an access price to a free natural resource which permits the depreciation of a resource without requirements of restoration.

The argument is both immediate and long-term. In the short run, over-fishing, the pressure of intensive agriculture on soil quality, and of industrial demand on natural forests are all depleting key resources in ways that the economists' formula of 'price system + new technology' has commonly hastened rather than reversed. To take only one example, the European Environment Agency estimates that five tonnes of soil per capita are being lost annually as the result of erosion.[23] Soil content in Italy has been halved in the past twenty years. Globally the world is estimated to have lost a quarter of its topsoil over the past fifty years. Desertification in China has come within forty miles of Beijing and is advancing at the rate of two miles a year. In this context, the use of composted organic wastes for agriculture is not just a question of carbon sequestration but of returning biomass to the soil and restoring the nutrient cycle.

The case is not confined to these immediate issues. As those in the Limits to Growth tradition point out, even if new technology extends the stock of recoverable mineral resources, or switches to new ones, the continued expansion of the current mode of industrial production and its extension to less developed countries, threatens many longstanding ecosystems without offering an adequate alternative.[24] As Schumpeter pointed out, capitalism has always advanced through creative destruction. In many of the central issues of the environment, destruction is running ahead of creation. From this perspective, the issue of climate change is only one example of a more general ecosystem phenomenon.

The policy question is how to reduce the intensity of resource use faster than the countervailing pressure of the growth of demand. Part of the answer lies in the way primary production is carried out (through the reduction of artificial fertilisers and pesticides in agriculture, for example, or clear cut logging); part in the dematerialisation of production and in changes in consumption. But there is also the question of the reduction and reuse of waste. At any one time, waste accounts for the majority of material flows. Until recently it was treated as a leftover from useful production. But it is clear that any strategy to reduce resource pressures has to address the volume of waste and what is done with it.

The size of these flows is only now being calculated. The World Resources Institute led an international team that traced the flows of 55 materials in 500 use streams (covering 95% of the weight of materials in the economy) for four leading OECD economies (the USA, Japan, the Netherlands and Germany). They found that the total materials requirement in these countries was 45 to 85 metric tonnes per person and that of this between 55% and 75% takes the form of waste materials that are discarded in the course of production (such as mining overburden, agricultural waste or material removed for infrastructural works).[25] They termed these 'hidden resources' since they do not enter the market economy save as a cost of disposal or restoration. They can be reduced by lowering the demand for the marketed resources to which they are attached, or by lowering the ratio of waste to primary marketed resources, or by reclaiming value from what would otherwise be waste. The same applies to waste from secondary production and to post-consumption waste: it has to be either reduced or 'revalorised' through recycling.

Waste – both in its process of generation and its treatment –

thus takes a central place in strategies to reduce the material footprint of industrialised economies. Every aluminium can recycled not only means that the need for new aluminium is reduced, but that the waste (and energy) associated with bauxite mining, as well as alumina and aluminium production, is also avoided. These are referred to as the upstream benefits of recycling. They represent avoided materials production, avoided wastes and avoided energy.

Resource productivity is becoming a major theme of environmental policy. The UK Cabinet Office has published a study on the subject.[26] The European Environment Agency has just produced the first collection of data on European primary resource productivity. Environmental engineers and scientists have been discovering ways in which resource efficiency can be discontinuously increased. Amory Lovins, one of the principal proponents of the new 'materials revolution', sees the scope for using resources ten to a hundred times more productively, and increasing profitable opportunities in the process.[27] He and other members of the Factor Four and Factor Ten clubs suggest that if the first industrial revolution was centred around increases in labour productivity, the next frontier will be materials productivity.

A number of national and international bodies (including the OECD Council at Ministerial level) have proposed a goal of increasing materials productivity by a factor of ten within a generation, and the Austrian Government has adopted this in its National Environmental Plan. (The equivalent Dutch plan has a more modest target of a four-fold increase in materials productivity, and the German one has a 2.5-fold improvement.)[28]

Improving materials productivity through recycling conserves materials as well as the energy embodied in them. The Dutch Government forecasts that half of the energy efficiency gains it will make up to 2010 will be the result of improved materials productivity. The MARKAL researchers estimate that materials reduction in Western Europe – following increases in penalties for carbon use – would contribute emission reductions of 800 million tonnes of CO2 equivalent (compared to the current European emission level of 5.1 billion tonnes).[29] Materials savings and energy savings thus go hand in hand.

A turning point in the waste industry

Over the past ten years these environmental imperatives have provoked a response which was at first pragmatic and particular, aimed principally at identified problems of pollution. But in recent years its scope has widened, to the causes of pollution on the one hand and to the gathering global concerns of climate change, ecosystem depletion and resource productivity on the other.

Waste has suddenly become an issue too important to be left to the waste industry. It is seen no longer as simply a sectoral matter – though the waste industry itself has been put under pressure to change. Rather, waste like energy and water is now recognised as pervasive, connecting as it does to every sector of the economy. It raises questions about the toxicity of modern materials and the profligacy with which mass production uses up non-renewable resources.

As the questions have widened, so has the response. There has been a shift from the concentration on pollution control to a broader policy of 'Zero Waste'. 'Zero Waste' as a concept has only recently been applied to waste management. But it has already built up a momentum which promises to transform not just the waste industry but material production itself. In a way that could not have been predicted in the 1980s, the redefinition of waste promises to be, along with the information and knowledge revolution, one of the defining features of the post-industrial era.

II Zero Waste

Fair and foul

At one level the term 'Zero Waste' appears to be a contradiction in terms. Just as there can be no light without shadow, so useful matter, to have meaning, requires its opposite – useless waste. Or, to put it another way, if waste is defined as matter in the wrong place, then eliminating waste would take with it the possibility of matter being in the right place. If waste didn't exist we would have to invent it.

And that of course has been part of the problem. Waste has been seen as the dark side, as that against which we define the good. It has been the untouchable in the caste system of commodities. The idea that waste could be useful, that it should come in from the cold and takes its place at the table of the living, is one that goes far beyond the technical question of what possible use could be made of this or that. It challenges the whole way we think of things and their uses, about how we define ourselves and our status through commodities, by what we cast out as much as by what we keep in.[30]

There have been two currents that have sought to give waste a new identity. The first is longstanding. It combines the puritan and the utilitarian. It takes the view that nothing useful should be wasted. Overriding the personal usefulness of things, it seeks other uses as a way of preserving their inherent value – particularly the value that comes from the labour that made them. The work ethic finds its reflection in the commitment to recycling, one reason why recycling has always been strongest in northern Protestant Europe.

The other current is more recent. It is the environmental. Here waste is redefined in terms of its role in natural cycles. On this basis it turns the tables on conventional distinctions. Instead of the value of commodities and waste being defined in terms of personal utility, it looks at them both in terms of recyclability. Good waste is that which can be recycled. The test of commodities is whether they can become good waste. The problem of waste disposal is replaced by the problem of phasing out those materials which are hazardous and which cannot be recycled. The issue is not to get rid of them when they are finished but to avoid producing them in the first place. Environmentalists have recast the opposition of good things and bad waste into a question of good waste and bad things.

For both these currents Zero Waste has been an aspiration. The environmental imperatives discussed earlier are now creating a pressure for Zero Waste to be made real. The decisive forces to link aspiration and practice together have come from two quarters: the environmental movement itself which has inspired a new generation of practical experimentation and design, and the world of industry and its rethinking of production.

The term 'Zero Waste' originates from the latter. In the past twenty years it has been increasingly adopted as a goal for commercial waste minimisation. It is an extension of the Japanese-based ideas of total quality management (TQM) into the environmental field.

One of the early TQM concepts was 'zero defects'. This involves the establishment of practices that allow a firm to eliminate all defects. It is incremental in approach, with intermediate 'stretch targets', directed at the pursuit of optima rather than restricting progress to choices between alternative known solutions. It has been extraordinarily successful, with producers like Toshiba achieving results as low as one defect per million.

The same approach has been applied within a TQM framework to zero emissions and Zero Waste. As the Japanese planning ministry recently put it: 'Waste is an un-Japanese concept.' Japanese firms have been in the lead in adopting Zero Waste policies, with Honda (Canada) reducing its waste by 98% within a decade, and Toyota aiming for the zero target by 2003. The puritan aspiration is becoming an industrial reality.

Over the past five years, the idea of Zero Waste has been transferred to the municipal field. In 1996 Canberra became the first city to adopt a Zero Waste target (for 2010). Its example has inspired a municipal Zero Waste movement in New Zealand. Some Californian authorities, having achieved their initial targets of 50% waste reduction, are now moving to the next phase of Zero Waste. The approach adopted is to set demanding targets in terms of what has to be done, which then become challenges at every level of the organisation. As with TQM more generally, Zero Waste is at the same time a long-term goal and a particular methodology about how to get there.

As an approach to municipal waste it has three distinguishing characteristics:

- its starting point is not the waste sector as such but the systems of production and consumption of which waste forms a part. It is an industrial systems view rather than a view from one (the final) part of the economic chain;

- it approaches the issue of waste and its redefined role from the perspective of the new industrial paradigm – looking at it in terms of the knowledge economy and complex multiple product systems;

- it proposes a different model of environmental policy and of the process of industrial change.

Intensive recycling and composting remain at the centre of Zero Waste as a strategy. Yet its impact goes beyond these approaches, to the contribution of the waste sector to the wider project of industrial redesign.

The three prime goals of Zero Waste are a direct response to the environmental imperatives currently pressing on the waste industry:

(i) zero discharge

First it is a policy to reduce to zero the toxicity of waste. Such a policy, applied to water and termed zero discharge, was first actively pursued by the US and Canadian governments in the Great Lakes Water Quality Agreement of 1978. The International Joint Commission that oversees the progress of the Agreement defined it as follows:

"Zero Discharge means just that: halting all inputs from all human sources and pathways to prevent any opportunity for persistent toxic substances to enter the environment as a result of human activity. To prevent such releases completely their manufacture, use, transport and disposal must stop; they simply must not be available. Thus zero discharge does not mean less than detectable. It also does not mean the use of controls based on best available technology, best management practices or similar means of treatment that continue to allow the release of some residual chemicals."[31]

The idea of zero discharge was adopted (without the term) by the fifteen-country Oslo and Paris (OSPAR) Commission on the North East Atlantic in 1992 and by the Barcelona Convention on the Mediterranean in October 1993. This is how the OSPAR agreement put it:

"Discharges and emissions of substances which are toxic, persistent and bio-accumulative, in particular organohalogen substances, and which could enter the marine environment, should, regardless of their anthropogenic source, be reduced by the year 2000 to levels that are not harmful to man or nature with the aim of their elimination."

What is being said here is that substances that are toxic, which resist the natural processes of material breakdown and recycling, but rather accumulate to ever higher levels in the environment, should be eliminated. Reducing their discharge means only slowing their rate of accumulation. The goal must therefore be zero discharge through phasing out the production of the substances in question. In the words of the Agreement, 'They simply must not be available.'

The three Agreements all relate to the pollution of water. The pollution can come about in the process of production, use or disposal. It can pass directly to water (through water emissions in production for example) or indirectly via the air, or through run-offs and leaching to water from land. Solid wastes are one form that can transfer or increase the pollution.

Zero Waste as applied to solid waste carries with it the idea of reducing with the aim of eliminating the presence in wastes of substances 'harmful to man or nature'. It means reducing all forms of toxic waste entering the waste stream, and methods of treatment of waste materials which result in 'persistent toxic substances' entering the environment.

Zero Waste goes beyond the existing practices of separating out hazardous materials and subjecting them to more stringent disposal requirements, and of basing required levels of control (at hazardous and non-hazardous sites) on assimilative capacities and acceptable discharges. It does not stop with end-of-pipe controls. Such controls have faced repeated problems of regulatory infringement, of the switching of pollution from one means of discharge to another (as with incinerator air emission controls, where toxicity is switched from air to ash and to the water used for plant cleaning), and of the lack of controls on emissions whose long-term health effects are not yet known (such as micro-particulates). Rather the aim of Zero Waste, like zero discharge, is to track to the source the cause of toxicity and control it by substituting non-toxic alternatives.

As such, Zero Waste invokes the principle of Clean Production. Clean Production aims to phase out the generation and use of toxic chemicals and materials by redesigning products and manufacturing methods to eliminate the inputs of toxic substances.[32] It targets toxic substances such as long-lived radioactive materials and heavy metals, which have been persistent sources of waste pollution. Its current priority is the phasing out of organohalogens, the substances specifically targeted in the OSPAR and Barcelona Agreements. Of the three principal organohalogens – organochlorines, organobromines and organoiodines – it is organochlorines that are the focus of immediate attention (the twelve priority pollutants of the current Stockholm Convention all being organochlorines). Waste products containing organochlorines (such as PVC, solvents, and PCBs) are the source of dioxins produced by incineration, and of many of the toxic effects of landfills.

(ii) zero atmospheric damage

The second principle of Zero Waste is the reduction to zero of atmospheric damage resulting from waste. With respect to climate change the first issue is the reduction of methane emissions from landfills. This would largely be ended by prohibiting the landfilling of untreated biological waste. Article 6 of the EU's Landfill Directive contains such a provision which should be interpreted – from the environmental rather than the bureaucratic perspective – as requiring forms of treatment of residual waste which reduce the fermentability of the organic fraction to no more than 10% of its initial level. Zero Waste here means zero untreated waste to landfill.[33]

A wider question is how the management of waste can help restore the carbon balance. Zero Waste in this context does not (and could not) mean eliminating CO2 emissions but rather:

- the minimisation of the loss of energy embodied in existing materials and products and of the use of fossil fuel energy for the process of recycling;

- Zero Waste of carbon that could be sequestered through the return of composted organic materials to the soil.

As far as CO_2 is concerned, the central operational concept of relevance is environmental opportunity cost. This means estimating environmental costs in terms of the net environmental benefits forgone by choosing one method of production or disposal over another. The net environmental benefits of incineration, for example, cannot be estimated solely by comparing the energy recovered from burning waste with the environmental cost of the incineration process, but must take account of the net environmental benefits foregone were that waste to be recycled.

Estimating these environmental costs and benefits is the subject of life cycle analysis (LCA), which normally compares alternative methods of disposal (landfill and incineration) with recycling. It aims to show where, in what respects and for what materials it is preferable to use one method of waste treatment rather than another. It has become a new form of environmental accountancy.

But there are problems in the way in which LCA has been used. It has been static, considering solely an existing pattern of alternative resource use. It does not take account of potential patterns that may emerge in the future. For instance, it takes time for new markets to develop for recycled materials, and as a result early recyclers often have to ship their materials long distances to find existing processors. Over time processors move closer to the recycled materials and the environmental (and financial) costs of transport fall. A dynamic approach looks at the results of life cycle analysis to see how the environmental costs of recycling can be reduced in order to maximise the net benefits from conserving resources.

Nor do LCAs look beyond the product to the systems of which they are a part, and how those systems can be transformed in order to reduce negative environmental impacts. LCAs tend to be narrow and incremental. Instead of being used as a means for judging between alternative methods of waste treatment, they should rather be seen as a tool in the design process of recycling and the production systems of which recycling forms a part.[34]

Zero Waste adopts a dynamic systems perspective to the conservation of embodied energy. It aims to maximise the net energy saving from recycling, by finding ways of cutting down energy use in the recovery and reprocessing of materials, and of substituting renewable for fossil fuel energy to produce the energy required.

Leading recycling jurisdictions have developed reprocessing close to the point of recycling (reviving urban manufacturing in the process). They have promoted renewables to produce energy for reprocessing, and in the UK and Italy, used low energy electric vehicles for recycling and organics collection. The goal is to use zero non-renewable energy in the process of recycling in order to achieve Zero Waste of the 'grey energy' contained in the recyclables.

(iii) zero material waste

Third, Zero Waste aims to eliminate material waste itself. Most tangibly, this means an end to all waste for disposal. No material would be discarded as worthless, instead a use would be found for it. Thus builders' rubble which was not recoverable for construction could as a last resort be used for land restoration (like much quarry waste).

This pragmatic goal highlights the potential value of waste, and the importance of phasing out the treatment of mixed waste streams. Its limitation is that it cannot distinguish the relative environmental (or financial) value of alternative uses of the materials. Thus metals recovered magnetically after incineration are of low quality, but their reuse used to be classed as recycling alongside high quality metals recovered through source separation. The definition of Zero Waste in this context then turns on the definition of use, which can be made so wide that it undercuts the goal of conserving resources.

To the pragmatic definition should then be added a concept of Zero Waste that entails the maximisation of material conservation. This perspective is embodied in the concept of material cycles developed by two of the most innovative Zero Waste thinkers, Michael Braungart and William McDonough. They distinguish two main cycles:

- the biological cycle for products that are composed of biodegradable materials called biological nutrients that can be safely returned to the environment at the end of a product's useful life and contribute to the rebuilding of depleted soils;

- the technical cycle composed of 100% reusable materials called technical nutrients designed in such a way that they can remain in closed loop systems throughout their life cycle.

The residual 'unmarketable products... those that cannot be used or consumed in an environmentally sound way and for which no safe recycling technology exists,' should in the long run no longer be produced.[35]

The biological cycle is renewable, whereas the technical cycle comprises non-renewable resources. One strategy they suggest is to develop new biological materials that substitute for non-renewable ones. The replacement of oil-based plastics by vegetable-based ones is an example (as in the case of plastic bags) or of bio-plastics for steel (Volkswagen is now making car doors out of plant-derived plastics). In cases where the resource and financial cost of recycling is high (e.g. plastic bags) the product can be returned as a nutrient to the soil.

A second strategy – which is inherent in this concept of cycles – is that of sustaining quality. In the biological cycle, it is critical that the 'bio waste' is returned to the soil in a way that enhances rather than degrades it. Contamination and mineral balance are central to issues of soil quality. Compost that is suitable only for landfill cover represents a degradation in terms of the reproducibility of the cycle.

The same applies to technical nutrients. There are technical cycles that continuously degrade the materials, such as the use of recycled PET bottles for garden furniture. Braungart and McDonough refer to this as 'downcycling' and see it as characteristic of most current waste diversion practices. 'Reduction, reuse and recycling are actually only slightly less destructive (than landfills and incinerators) because they slow down the rates of contamination and depletion rather than stopping these processes.' The environmental goal should be recycling and up-cycling: 'the return to industrial systems of materials with improved, rather than degraded, quality'.[36]

The idea of up-cycling suggests that we should talk of material spirals rather than cycles. Zero Waste becomes a question of not merely conserving the resources that went into the production of particular materials, but adding to the value embodied in them by the application of knowledge in the course of their recirculation. An example given by Michael Braungart is the use of rice husks. Originally they posed a waste disposal problem in Asia because they were incombustible. Braungart developed new uses for them, first as a substitute for polystyrene as a packaging material for electronic goods and then, after that use, as a fire-resistant building material. In this case, previously unacknowledged natural properties of a material were identified that allowed them to be revalued as they were applied to a succession of uses.

Projects to realise the value of secondary materials have generated a new technology of alternative uses as these materials are studied for their properties and then substituted for existing primary-material-based processes. One of many examples is the use of rubber crumb made from old motor tyres to make basketball courts in the USA. The extra spring in the court has reduced the knee stress on professional basketball players, extending their careers.

Cyclical Production, the proposition of reconceptualising (and redesigning) the economic process in terms of two cycles – of biological and technical nutrients – is one of the central ideas of Zero Waste. Its focus is on the material life cycle and the conditions for materials to flow through a succession of uses ('from cradle to cradle' rather than 'from cradle to grave').

A second key concept is Sufficient Production. This addresses the amount of materials and energy consumed (and potential waste produced) in a single cycle. It deals with the material intensity of production, the reduction of extractive and manufacturing waste, the lifetime of products, the effectiveness of their uses, and the way in which they can achieve their desired outcome in consumption with less material input. It shifts the strategic emphasis from efficiency to sufficiency, and to how the productive systems and the products they contain can be reconfigured to cut the material flows required.

If Cyclical Production focuses on the qualitative features of materials from the perspective of recycling, Sufficient Production highlights ways in which the quantities of materials and potential waste can be reduced. Both apply to energy as well as to material 'sufficiency'. Together with Clean Production they form the three central industrial pillars of Zero Waste.

Zero Waste is a consequence as much as a cause of these shifts in production. The pollution problems of waste management may have triggered innovation, as is the case with the movement for Clean Production. Waste management also has a role to play in re-establishing the material cycles. Yet now the drivers for change are shifting back up the pipe. Manufacturers and industrial designers are moving to the centre of the stage both to ensure technical and economic recyclability of materials, and to reduce the need for production and the use of materials in the first place.

This is an important point, since too often the quantity and toxicity of waste has been held to be the responsibility of waste managers, and within their capacity to control. Yet waste managers are for the most part the passive recipients of problems which have been produced elsewhere.

Responsibility has been passed down the line and ended up with them because there was nowhere else for it to go. Their job has been to get rid of these problems as safely and cheaply as possible and now, when the limitations of this old system have become apparent, they are being asked to devise an alternative system for reducing and neutralising the environmental damage done by waste.

The task is an impossible one. The keepers of the terminus cannot be expected to redesign the system. They are strangers to the industrial world. They are structurally and culturally far removed from design. Once waste is connected back to the wider industrial system – through reuse and recycling – the axis of responsibility for waste shifts from the waste industry back to those who produced it. They in turn are in the best position to do something about it. If waste is re-conceptualised as a resource, then it is the specialists in resources – who produce them, apply them and discard them – who should take responsibility for transforming the way they are used.

A new way of seeing

Zero Waste has multiple perspectives – of clean production, of atmospheric protection and resource conservation. Taken together these provide a new way of analysing waste – a new way of seeing. Although it is a contributor to environmental degradation, waste cannot be treated in isolation. Waste is only the final stage of a much wider chain of production and consumption in which the problems associated with it are rooted. In this sense waste is a symptom as much as a cause, a sign of failure in the design and operation of the material economy. It provides an insight into deeper structures, as well as an opportunity for changing them.

For these reasons, while Zero Waste provides the basis for reformulating policies for waste management, it is not just about cutting waste going for disposal, whether landfill or incineration. Its aim is the restoration of pre-industrial circuits – the biological circuit of organic materials and the technical circuit of inorganic ones – using post-industrial means. It offers a way in which the negative detritus of an earlier era is transformed – through ecodesign – into a positive nutrient for clean production. Zero Waste is a manifesto for the redesign of the material economy, and at the same time, it is a set of tactics for realising its principles in practice.

It is also a description of what is already happening. Over the past decade a change has taken place in the industrial landscape that has been too little noticed. The change is occurring in two fields – in the way waste is managed on the one hand, and the way it is produced on the other. The first is creating a new waste industry, the second a new industrial approach to materials. Both are part of a wider green industrial revolution.

III **The growth of recycling**

First the waste industry. It has since its inception been primarily concerned with mixed waste rather than recycling. Although there has always been some measure of recycling, it has been a residual function, commonly carried out by processing industries, or, where wages are low, by totters, scavengers and nightsoil collectors. In industries where there were relatively homogeneous waste flows and materials with a good resale value (like metals and paper) the waste was either recycled within the plant or transferred through merchants to mills that could handle it. The problem came with low value waste, and with mixed waste streams from which it was difficult to recover usable materials.

Municipal waste was particularly intractable. Local authorities would put out recycling bring banks and even run a newspaper collection, but municipal recycling rarely averaged more than 10%. The remainder, like most industrial and commercial waste, was bulked up and disposed of in the cheapest way possible. Waste and those who managed it were marginal to the economy.

Now the demand is for the opposite. It is recycling which is being moved to the centre of the stage, with residual waste banished to the wings. The turnaround has been most rapidly achieved in the commercial sector. In Copenhagen, for example the proportion of construction and demolition waste that is recycled has gone from 10% to 90% in less than a decade, and over half (51%) of industrial and commercial waste is now recycled. In Canada offices were diverting 70-80% of their waste within six months after simple recycling systems were introduced. Large events, like the Olympic Games in Atlanta, found that they could recycle 85% of waste produced. Schools, prisons, shops and hospitals have achieved similar levels.

The greatest challenge has been the municipal sector: mixed waste from thousands, even millions of people.

But here, too, the advance has been of a kind that few would have predicted ten years ago. A few communities have reached the levels common for commercial waste – 70-80%. Elsewhere, '50%' jurisdictions are now becoming commonplace. Cities, regions and even countries have passed through the 50% recycling barrier, the point at which residual waste becomes a minority share.

In North America:

- California, with a recycling rate of 10% in 1989, passed legislation requiring all its municipalities to reach 50% diversion from disposal by 2000. They reached 42% by the target date and expect to have hit 50% by the end of 2001. A majority of the 304 cities and counties in the state now have recycling rates of 50% or more;

- the USA as a whole raised its recycling rate from 8% in 1990 to 32% in 2000, with six states reaching 40% or above;

- Canada made 50% diversion by 2000 a national goal. Nova Scotia was the first province to hit the target by 2000, with its capital, Halifax, registering a level of 60%. Leading municipalities have now reached levels of 70% diversion.

In Australasia:

- Canberra has reached a level of 59% of municipal diversion and is shortly to introduce an organics collection scheme which will take it a further large step forward;

- in New Zealand, 8 of the 78 municipalities have already reached the 50% target.

In Europe:

- a growing number of states and regions have passed the 50% mark, including: German länder like Baden

Wurttemberg, Lower Saxony and Saarland; Flanders (now at 54%); and Italy's Milan province, where 88 out of 180 municipalities have reached the target, with 32 of them now over 60% and five over 70%;

- whole countries are now approaching or surpassing the benchmark. Germany raised its municipal recycling rate from 12.5% in 1990 to 46% in 1996. It's level of waste as a whole fell by a third. The Netherlands, in spite of its stock of incinerators, has managed to switch the balance of its waste from landfill to recycling, achieving a municipal recycling rate of 46% by 1998 (and 70% for all waste). The highest national level has been reached in Switzerland, which now has a rate of 53%.

These changes, when achieved at a national level within so short a time, are remarkable given the complexity of the new collection and sorting systems required and the quite different modes of operation for intensive recycling and mixed waste disposal. What they have established is that for any locality or region 50% diversion from disposal is readily achievable, usually within six to eight years, even without a new waste regulatory regime being fully in place.

The 1990s saw a head of steam arising at the municipal level for intensive recycling and composting, and the amassing of a body of experience in how to deliver it. The decade showed the economic significance of the new systems in practice, as they generated substantial numbers of new collection and sorting jobs[37] and also prompted the expansion of a wide range of processing industries. Institutions for finance developed, as well as advisory support for collectors, material sales and market development. In short, the 1990s saw the birth of a new industry and a new profession.

The industry is still in its early stages. It still bears the imprint of the refuse industry – with capital intensive sorting plant, large vehicles, and wheeled bins with automatic lifts. Some places have responded to the recycling challenge by collecting mixed waste as usual and trying to recover materials through centralised sorting (in so-called dirty Materials Reclamations Facilities - MRFs), using screening and magnetic extraction, or through mixed waste composting (a method in which non-organic materials are partially separated out from the organics, leaving a low quality compost residue).

A step forward from this has been to collect waste in two streams – a wet and a dry – composting the former and sorting the latter either by hand or through the application of increasingly complex sorting technology. More commonly, separate dry recycling collections are run in parallel with the main weekly collection, handling a limited number of materials separated at source. Germany has gone one step further with separate collections of packaging, organics, paper and residuals, each using similar set-out and collection technologies, and processed in centralised facilities.

All these are examples of recycling using the old methods. This is not unusual at points of industrial transition, as when the first cars located their drivers high up at the back, where a coachman used to sit to control the horses. But the old methods are often ill suited to their new tasks. Mixed waste systems have low recovery rates and yield poor material quality and the conditions for those working in the central sorting facilities are unsustainably hazardous.

The German systems have much better recovery rates but they are high cost, they entail expensive sorting technology, and are transport intensive. In the end these systems are self-limiting, either because of the quantity of recyclable material they can recover or the level of their costs. In either case they risk putting a technical or economic cap on the recycling rates that can be achieved.[38]

Yet in many places the barriers presented by the old ways of the waste business have been broken open. There is now a wave of innovation in the technical, organisational and economic structures of the industry that is both lowering costs and increasing recovery rates. The outlines of a new recycling economy are emerging which provide the conditions for the further advance towards Zero Waste.

This economy has three distinguishing characteristics:

- *flexible production systems.* It is replacing the single flow management of mass waste with flexible systems for handling multiple streams of good quality materials;

- *the core role of the social economy.* It recognises householders as key producers within the wider economic circuit of recycling, and is developing the incentives, knowledge and institutions appropriate to voluntary labour;

- *reconnecting to markets.* It is reorienting an industry that has hitherto been entirely dependent on public funding, to one that supplies materials to commercial processors and recycling services for a wide spectrum of waste producers.

Flexible recycling systems

The change in the system of collection and logistics required by recycling – from a single flow of materials to multiple flows – is similar to that which has been taking place in other manufacturing and service industries over the past 20 years. It lies at the heart of the new flexible manufacturing systems first introduced in Japanese manufacturing which have since spread throughout the world and to many service sectors.

Waste in this context is a latecomer, and the pioneers of intensive recycling reflect many of the features of this new industrial paradigm. They often come from areas whose economies have already made the transition: from the west coast and sections of the east coast of the USA and Canada; from the European regions celebrated for their dynamic manufacturing networks in the 'third Italy', Germany and the industrial districts in Spain; and from Australasia.

Flexible manufacturing entails a shift from the dedicated

machinery of mass production to general-purpose machines. It has turned the principles of FW Taylor and Scientific Management on their head, decentralising operational control to frontline workers, and re-skilling them. It has also involved the development of complex management information systems to keep track of the multiple flows, and to provide the data necessary for statistical production control by both the operatives and the technical support staff. Table 1 below summarises a number of key differences between the old paradigm of mass production and the new paradigm of flexible specialisation.[39]

Many of the features of mass production can be recognised in the traditional system of waste management and its methods of recycling. Most local authority waste departments and waste firms have extended vertical hierarchies of control. The role of the dustman or the recycling collector/sorter remains an epitome of unskilled labour (in some cases the sorting function being designed for the mentally impaired). Planning is separated from execution (in one UK case by no less than nine layers of authority). Investment is directed towards hardware not software. Systems are set up to feed large pieces of capital equipment (large MRFs with high capacity sorting of both plastics and paper, using electronic recognition technology). Scale still dominates over scope.

The 'smart' recycling systems, by contrast, combine the characteristics of the knowledge economy (design, multi-skilling, branding, advanced management information systems) with the technologies and organisational forms of flexible manufacturing.

Table 1

Mass Production (Fordism)	Flexible Specialisation (Post-Fordism)
Single product flow	Multi-product flow
Dedicated machinery	General purpose machinery
Push through	Pull through
High stocks	Just-in-Time production
Lengthy design and pre-production testing	Multiple products tested on the market
High reworks	Zero defects
Unskilled, single task labour	Multi skilled, multi-task labour
Division of planning, control and execution	Greater front line autonomy and continuous improvement
Pyramidal structures with vertical lines of command and reporting	Flat structures with horizontal as well as vertical linkages
Closed organisations	Open structures with multiple external networks
Price determined sub-contracting	Innovation-based subcontracting
Fixed capital-intensive	Knowledge-intensive

They have the following characteristics:

- *multiple services.* Collection moves from a standardised weekly model to multiple services geared to the time requirements of the particular waste stream. There is a new waste calendar (combining simplicity with the seasons) with weekly collections of dry recyclables, alternating fortnightly collections of food waste and residuals, monthly week-end collections of green waste, and quarterly collections of seasonal, durable or hazardous items (Christmas trees, clothing, spring cleaning clear-outs).

- *customised collection systems.* Services, vehicles and containers are designed to suit particular types of housing: in suburban areas and small towns multi-compartment vehicles have been effectively used; in dense inner city areas small pedestrian controlled vehicles (PCVs) with builders bags as compartments can be used (an innovation from the UK), or micro pick-ups for food waste and dry recyclables (an Italian scheme); in rural areas co-collection, as adopted by North American recyclers, allows commingled dry recyclables to be picked up with residual waste one week, and organics the next.

- *general-purpose equipment.* Vehicles are designed for multiple functions, adapting the principle of the container and pallet to the needs of recycling (flat-backed trucks with multiple mini-containers provide the flexibility that many multi-compartment vehicles lack). One of the features of modern flexible systems is the central importance of low cost switching, in this case the ease of transfer between types of vehicle (from a feeder vehicle to a compactor, for example, without the need for a transfer station).

- *decentralisation.* Sorting and logistics is redesigned away from a centralised hub and spoke model, to decentralised nodes and a 'latticed web' pattern of material movements. For example, the shift to small vehicles means that they can be stored in local garages and a measure of sorting can be conducted locally or at the kerbside, with materials stored at sub-depots in small containers for eventual transportation. Each collection round develops a greater operational and logistical autonomy.

- *de-scaling and modularising material processing.* Many processing industries have found economic ways of descaling production – notably the expansion of mini-mills in paper production and steel, and of micro-chemical plants. Commonly processes requiring scale are separated off, so that other processes can be decentralised, through sub-assemblies, and specialised preparation plants. For recycling, small, widely distributed processing centres reduce transport and encourage local 'loops' or cycles. Closed vessel micro-composters serve the same purpose, being able to economically process waste from a tower block or village. They are modular and can be located at civic amenity (CA) sites, parks, in the grounds of a hospital or beside a fishing port (see inset 1).

- *multi-skilling.* Collectors take centre stage in Zero Waste recycling: they are the frontline interface with householders (or firms); they provide a channel of advice and information; they analyse the data from their rounds and are responsible for improvements (houses passed, participation rates, levels of contamination). In addition to sorting they may also be responsible for some local processing, such as in-vessel composting. The pioneers here have been environmentalists who have set up recycling and composting schemes and who represent a new kind of 'green-collar worker'.

- *central service support.* 'Head office' services are geared to support the frontline staff (from standardised management information systems to the provision and maintenance of equipment, social marketing materials, and the administration of secondary material markets).

- *redefining management.* In the most advanced schemes senior management has changed its functions from day-to-day control to strategy, market development, system design, problem solving assistance, finance and recruitment and training.

- *stock management and gearing supply to demand.* Just-in-Time principles can only partially be applied in recycling since programmes are constrained by their function of recovering materials which would otherwise be discarded as waste. Yet recycling does play a role in managing the cyclical flow between discards and reuse. It influences the supply of materials in response to market demand: through campaigns to expand the supply of particular materials (effectively reducing the stock of the

Inset 1

Vertical compost unit

A vertical closed vessel compost unit in Waitakere, New Zealand. Waitakere is town of 80,000 households within the Aukland region. The unit has a capacity of 14,000 tonnes a year, using ten chambers, which allows different qualities of feedstock to be processed separately.

The technology was developed by microbiologists in New Zealand. Temperatures reach at least 80 degrees, which encourages the development of pyrophilic bacteria that act as a bio-filter for the exhaust gases from the compost. As a result, there is no odour, so that the plants can be sited in dense urban areas, within 50m metres of housing.

Since the equipment is modular, it can be geared to the size of the area served. A single unit with a capacity of some 1,250-1,400 tonnes, would service the organic waste from a town or urban estate of 5,000 – 10,000 households, and require an hour a day to maintain its operation.

The Waitakere plant processes source separated organics and garden waste from households, and catering scraps from a scheme run by the council for local shops and restaurants. It sells the compost to a local landscaping firm, which mixes it with topsoil for use in new housing developments.

Plants of this kind have recently been established in the UK in Sheffield, North Lincolnshire and Bromley.

material held by the householder); and/or by stockholding or redirecting materials to alternative uses in the case of oversupply. Reuse centres cut their stocks, by the use of a database with internet access and the allocation of repair labour according to demand.

- *cybernetic planning*. Instead of the old system of waste planning, with long-term plans containing multiple uncertainties and linked to large scale capital investments that provide the 'skeleton' of the waste system, the new paradigm works on iterative short-, medium-and long-term plans, regularly revised in the light of experience, with flexible collection (and disposal) systems that can be rapidly reprogrammed to take account of unforeseen events.

The key words found in the 'post-industrial' recycling systems are flexibility, micro-processes, distributed knowledge, operational decentralisation, nested organisations and 'the present as laboratory'.

In sum, intensive recycling is transforming the waste industry in line with the wider industrial changes of the current era – applying the approaches and modes of operation of the knowledge economy and flexible manufacturing systems to waste. It has been found that the methods, skills, technologies and organisational forms necessary to achieve high levels of recycling performance have much in common with the new post-industrial economy, and at the same time the post-industrial economy is now taking on the issue of its own waste minimisation as part of the environmental reorientation of industrial production. The operational 'ecologies' of the two are remarkably similar.

Recycling as social economy

Successful recycling depends critically on the voluntary labour of the household. Whereas in the past householders had merely to put out their bin once a week, now they are asked to separate their waste and supply recyclables. They come to play a central role in production.

Furthermore they are unpaid. This presents an economic conundrum. Householders with a convenient, simple service (the dustbin or paladin) are being invited to engage in a more time-consuming service which, far from being paid for, commonly costs them more. Seen through the utilitarian lens, it is surprising that there is any voluntary participation at all in recycling schemes.

The answer of course is that recycling provides an opportunity to contribute to a wider social goal. It is an example of 'productive democracy', for which payment would be no more expected than it would for voting. This explains the remarkable popularity of recycling and the high participation rates of 80% or more that well run systems have achieved.

It also underlines the point that this is a 'value-led' service, that people engage in it because of its meaning. One of the characteristics of high diversion programmes is that many of them grew out of opposition to landfills and incinerators. It was the direct experience of 'old pollution' that drew in communities to the recycling alternative. It established recycling's environmental meaning. Successful programmes have always treated this 'meaning' as central and have organised their processes to reflect it.

Recyclers in North America look at the issue in terms of social marketing. From this perspective recycling is a brand. It is a word that carries with it an environmental and ethical meaning. Like any brand it has been attacked by those with whom it competes (the traditional waste industry) and it has been subject to 'brand degradation' where its practices fail to match up to its principles. Nothing does more to damage recycling than the discovery that recycled materials are finishing up in landfills or that sorting mixed waste in dirty MRFs causes as great a hazard for the workers involved as conventional dumping.

Market research analysts regard the rise of green and ethical consumption as part of a wider 'post-industrial' trend in which commodities are valued for the ethic they represent as well as the services they deliver. Large corporations recognise this and seek to associate themselves with ethical organisations and causes. Recycling is a paradigm case of an activity centred round 'meaning'. People are urged to buy recycled goods not because they are better (they are usually indistinguishable) but because they are less environmentally damaging. They are asked to set out their recycling box not because there is anything in it for them as individuals, but because it contributes to a social solution. It is 'other directed' rather than 'self directed', which is why recycling was so successful during the Second World War.

It also explains why so much social enterprise has grown up around recycling. Community collectors achieve the highest participation rates, followed by local authorities and private waste companies (in that order).[40] In Britain and France, social enterprise has pioneered the recycling of white goods, of furniture and more recently of electronics. There is a strong community composting network in the UK. In North America, grass roots recyclers have developed remarkably successful reuse centres which deal not just with waste but with goods (like textiles) which people do not want to waste. In New Zealand community enterprises have been at the centre of the expansion of recycling. As diversion expands, these functions may be taken over by private commercial enterprises, but their success has in part proved dependent on their being able to sustain goodwill.

The new recycling is in its essence a social as much as a technical economy. The leading programmes internationally have invested as much if not more in social marketing and education as they have in recycling vehicles. They have provided teams of compost advisers. They have invested in training so that the frontline collectors also act as advocates and sources of information. They have involved local communities in the planning of recycling-led waste systems, and in their monitoring. The social and environmental meaning of recycling has been a core criterion for decisions as diverse as collection technologies and the acceptance of sponsorship.

Recycling as market economy

If the social economy is one element of the new recycling, the market economy is another. From the late nineteenth century, household waste disposal has been defined as a public function to be provided free and paid for through taxation. The state took responsibility – on public health grounds – for its collection and disposal. High level recycling has changed this in two ways.

First, responsibility for waste – including household waste – is being transferred from the state to producers and consumers. The polluter is being made to pay. This has led both to the introduction of fees for household waste disposal (a reflection of increased consumer responsibility) and the establishment of recycling schemes by or on behalf of manufacturers or others held responsible for the waste (producer responsibility).

In some cases producers recycle their own products and materials through take-back schemes or, like some recycled paper mills, run their own collection schemes. In others, they have subcontracted the task of return and recycling to particular collectors. In the UK the 'obligated parties' under the packaging directive use intermediary brokering institutions to perform this function – the so-called packaging schemes. As the packaging targets increase, some of these schemes are looking for ways of securing sources of supply of recyclates through sub-contracting, as well as long-term contracts for demand.

In each instance the waste operators, whether public or private, find themselves no longer funded solely through the public purse, but through householder contributions and producer payments. The market for waste services, in short, is being fragmented and diversified.

Second, recyclers have become materials merchants facing commodity markets. As recycling increases so the value of recovered materials assumes ever greater importance in the economics of waste. This is straightforward, even if a challenge for a sector previously insulated from the market.

But one of the principal features of the high recycling programmes is that as material intermediaries, they have come to play a distinct function in the re-establishment of material cycles.

On the one hand they transmit the demands of the users of materials back down the chain, identifying problems originating in the initial production of the recycled materials (such as pathogens and heavy metals in food which are carried over into compost) and putting pressure on the producers to resolve them at source.

On the other they have acted as innovators in the use of materials, identifying multiple uses of recycled materials and developing new markets accordingly. Some of the most advanced recycling programmes (such as that in Washington State in the USA) have established market development units, staffed with engineers and material specialists to identify and market new uses for recovered materials.

What is emerging from these arrangements is the direct organisation of the material cycle, involving the producers and retailers of products, the recyclers and the reprocessors. This allows the technological and quality requirements of the reprocessors to be fed directly back down the line, and like the Japanese vertical production chains, for issues concerning the development of the chain as a whole to be discussed by all involved.

It is therefore not just a question of the marketisation of waste as a resource, but the introduction of a particular type of market. At first recyclers were secondary material merchants operating in national and international commodity markets. But as recycling has expanded, recyclers become key intermediaries, assuming the role of specialist suppliers of collection, separation and logistics within directly organised material cycles.

Towards Zero Waste

The above describes the key features of the emerging intensive recycling economy. I have referred to it as 'smart' recycling since it applies the principles of the knowledge economy and flexible manufacturing systems to the recovery and recirculation of materials. In its most challenging sector – municipal waste – it combines in a remarkably innovative way all three spheres of the economy – the household, the state and the market.

When the system is introduced in this way – quite apart from its reduced environmental impact – it is commonly a cheaper way of managing waste than the old disposal system. Although it is necessarily more expensive to run multiple collections rather than one, leading programmes have found ways of restricting the cost increases for separated collections of dustbin waste to as little as 20% above the single mixed waste system. The critical variables are the savings that can be made on residual collections once high recycling is established, the use of low cost/high productivity vehicles and bins for the separated waste, and the capture rate of materials. Against the increase in collection costs are set the savings from disposal on the one hand and the sale of materials on the other. The higher the disposal costs and the higher the sales income, the sooner will intensive recycling systems lead to budget savings.

These can be considerable. Seattle cut its waste budget by 8% in six years. In Quinte, Ontario, the savings reached 38% in eight years. In a recent survey of high recycling programmes in the USA, nine of the fourteen for which comparable cost data were available reduced their waste budgets through intensive recycling, and a further four would have done so if the rise in landfill costs had not offset the collection savings. The economics of Zero Waste should be seen as an opportunity, not a constraint.

For those at the bottom of the Zero Waste mountain it is hard to believe it can be climbed. There is incredulity that towns and cities, and even countries, are even halfway there, and have saved money in the process. The next section describes the routes they have taken. There is no single model, no one set way. But a broad pattern is emerging which makes it easier for those still looking up from below.

IV The Road to Zero Waste

1. Setting the compass

The first feature of all successful high diversion programmes is the strength of the idea. For a programme to have roots and direction it has to have a shared idea of its environmental and social purpose. Although individual incentives play a role, it is the common goals which are the raison d'être and generate the mobilising energy for the project. They also provide the criteria that inform waste strategies.

This is an important point for waste managers in the UK. Too often waste plans in this country have set as their primary tasks the meeting of EU and government targets and directives. This places local authorities in the role of a subordinate, whose goals and values are determined elsewhere. The danger is that the targets become detached from the intention behind them, so that an authority will be concerned more with meeting the targets than with whether the route they have chosen reflects underlying priorities.[41]

For those outside local government, particularly householders, who play a key role in the new waste arrangements both as voters and waste producers, bureaucratic objectives such as meeting government targets have less meaning than environmental objectives such as reduced toxicity and emissions of CO_2. It is not that government targets should not be met: the initial recycling targets are statutory and binding. It is rather that they should be seen as a consequence, not a prime reason, for any strategy.

Sustained political leadership has been particularly important in recycling for this reason, in articulating and keeping to the fore the central meaning of the programme. But it has also been important that the establishment of the programme is not treated simply as a technical matter, and that the broader values are internalised in its design and conduct. In order to achieve this, many programmes have been designed (and in some cases operated) in close partnership with the communities they serve.

2. Targets as staging posts

Once the overall goals are clear, targets have a context. They have often been a point of contest. Innovators want to set targets beyond the horizon. Bureaucracies prefer to remain well within it. But in terms of achieving high recycling, targets should be ambitious – so-called 'stretch targets' in order to encourage radical innovation. They should be set in relation to what is required. They embody the goals. In the words of Gerry Gillespie, one of the promoters of Zero Waste policies in Australia and New Zealand, the Americans and the Russians did not aim to send a man halfway to the moon. They were advised by their scientists on the potential feasibility of the project, but they were setting a goal not on the basis of existing levels of technology, but on what might be developed in the future.

Good targets reflect an impatience with the present. They then become the yardstick against which advance can be measured. Japanese manufacturers do not care how low the bar is to begin with. Their interest is in how high it can go, and with the closely observed ups and downs of the progress towards it.

High recyclers have set ambitious targets – usually 50%, in the first instance, to be achieved within a decade. Many found they reached that level more quickly, and target dates have been brought forward – to five years and even less. Individual municipalities find that they can reach 50% within two years of launching. For places still in the early stages of recycling, reaching 50% diversion in five years is a reasonable first stage target in the light of current experience and techniques.

In the long term, many places are now confident that they can reach much higher levels. In California, the 50+% municipalities are planning for 70-80% diversion, with some districts and cities (notably Del Norte and Santa Cruz) targeting Zero Waste. In Canada, districts like Quinte, that have reached 70%, are now planning for 85%. The Nova Scotia county of Annapolis Royal is aiming for Zero Waste by 2005. Zero Waste has now become the goal for 40% of all municipalities in New Zealand, following the lead of Canberra.

The above suggests that in addition to a first stage target of 50% within five years, further stretch targets should be set of 70% diversion within ten years, 85% in fifteen and Zero Waste in twenty.

3. The S-curve and the Pareto Principle

Behind these targets lies a proposition that the expansion of recycling follows an S-curve. The curve describes the fact that, after an initial slow growth, the recycling rate can climb steeply to 50% and 60%, and then continue at a slower rate as waste reduces towards zero. It is a description of the growth of individual recycling programmes to date.

The rationale reflects the Pareto Principle that a small number of causes are responsible for a large proportion (commonly 80%) of the effects. In the case of dustbin waste, five materials (organics, paper, glass, cans and textiles) account for 80% of the weight. For bulky waste taken to civic amenity sites (CA sites), 70% of the weight comprises three materials (organic waste, builders' waste and wood), with a further three materials taking the figure up to 80% (paper, metals and furniture). In broad terms, if an authority sets up a small number of core programmes that capture 80% of these '80% materials' from 80% of its residents, it will reach the first target of 50%.

Those authorities that have pursued intensive programmes of this kind have found that their household diversion rates rise rapidly to reach 50% or more, with commercial rates increasing even more sharply. This represents the steep part of the S-curve.

After that the household rate is pushed further by two factors. First participation and capture rates increase in the existing programmes, often aided by the introduction of user pay systems. Second, new materials are added to the collection and new programmes are started aimed at items that become significant in the residual stream. An example would be nappies, which account for 4% of the domestic dustbin, but 10% of the residual once a 60% target has been reached. The rate of expansion slows as programmes have to deal with the more difficult materials, and less participative households.

4. The four-stream system

The most common core programme for the first stage is described as the four-stream system, of which three streams represent dustbin waste:

- organic waste

- dry recyclables

- residual dustbin waste and a fourth stream represents:

- bulky goods

These all need to be dealt with separately, with further sub-divisions in each category. While in each case it may be possible to arrange for householders, firms and institutions to process their own waste (as in the case of on-site composting) or to bring their waste to a common collection point (to recycling banks, civic amenity sites, shops for returnable bottles or to roadside Eurobins for residual waste in Mediterranean Europe), the core of the intensive recycling structure is kerbside collection.

The first priority is organic waste. This makes up 30-50% of dustbin waste throughout Europe, and in the UK 40% of civic amenity site waste. High levels of organic diversion will not only reduce the toxicity of landfill, it will propel municipalities towards the 50% target. Many

North American authorities that have reached 50% or more have done so without kitchen waste collections, relying rather on home composting programmes and the kerbside collection of garden waste. The same is true of Canberra in Australia. But home composting alone will never achieve the levels of diversion of doorstep food waste collections, so that for Zero Waste, a regular food waste pick-up is the first building block of the new system, with seasonal collections of that garden waste which cannot be composted at home.[42] Separate food waste collections have been the reason why so many Italian cities have reached 50%-plus targets of waste diversion within three years.

The second stream is dustbin dry recyclables. Kerbside collection of recyclables should aim to reach an average of 2.7kg per household passed per week within three years, and 4kg per household within eight years, yielding a dustbin recycling rate of 17-25%. The priority material is paper – both newspaper and magazines, and other mixed paper, followed by textiles, cans and lastly glass.

The third stream is residual dustbin waste, which will dramatically fall in volume, and whose collection needs to be integrated with the organics and dry recycling collections. Within the residual stream, special arrangements are required to remove hazardous waste. Some is collected in bags attached to the dry recyclables collection (batteries and old pharmaceuticals for example). A growing number of municipalities have assigned special areas of their civic amenity sites for the full range of hazardous items that can be recycled or disposed of appropriately.

The three-stream system for the collection of dustbin waste is the core programme for intensive municipal recycling. In the spirit of smart recycling it does not necessarily mean three separate collections. In some cases two streams can be collected in separate compartments of the same vehicle. In others, there may be four or five collections: for food waste, garden waste, fibres and containers, and residuals. What matters is that the streams remain separate to avoid contamination.

In respect to the fourth stream, bulky waste, it is primarily handled throughout Europe, North America and Australasia via a small number of designated bring sites, often at landfills, supported by doorstep collections for those without cars or who live in rural areas. Recycling is relatively straightforward in this case, with residents and traders instructed to source-separate their waste and place it in the relevant containers. As a result, diversion rates of 60-70% can be rapidly achieved, provided that the layout of the sites is re-organised and sufficient green collar staff employed.

The problem with this system is that while it is cheap for local authorities, it is a major generator of traffic (accounting for nearly 1% of car traffic in outer London for example). There is an environmental case for introducing a more systematic doorstep collection scheme for bulk goods, as well as extending take-back systems through commercial delivery vehicles as producer responsibility regulations come onstream.

In the USA and Canada bring sites of this kind have been refashioned into recycling and reuse centres. They have become transfer sites for the recycling of consumer durables, as well as places of recreation – a market for reuse goods, an education centre and a waste museum.

The above four-stream system has been adopted for trade and institutional waste as well as waste from households, often using the same vehicles and facilities.

5. Mapping

Intensive recycling needs to give as much priority to mapping its waste as the nineteenth century General Staff in Prussia gave to mapping their territories. In the case of waste, the primary mapping will have three main parts:

- an analysis of the composition of waste

- an identification of the main sources and quantities of waste

- an audit of existing assets

(i) **waste composition**

In the era of mass waste, what mattered was not the composition of waste but its volume and weight. Increased awareness of pollution led to new classification of special and hazardous wastes, but these mainly applied to industries, not households. For the most part waste was waste. The issue was quantity not quality.

Incinerators were a partial exception. They did have an interest in the combustibility of their feedstock, and undertook periodic studies to distinguish the main elements of waste in relation to their calorific values. But the studies remained aggregated, with categories such as combustible and non-combustible, and with large residual categories such as 'miscellaneous' and 'fines'.

The starting point for Zero Waste has been disaggregation. Sorting techniques have been developed which can identify the composition of each of the waste streams, as mineralogists identify their metals. It has been found that an adequate analysis requires hand sorting. It cannot be done satisfactorily by machines. Hand sorting allows the breakdown of waste into fifty or more components, and gives the planners of recycling direct experience of the materials with which they are working. Like opinion polling, waste composition sampling is done regularly as a measure of progress and a guide to practice.

(ii) **estimating quantities**

In the past, mass waste has been measured at the point at which it has to be paid for – at the point of transfer and/or disposal (although in the UK as in other parts of

Europe by no means all landfills have weighbridges). Yet the lorries that bring in the waste often have mixed contents from different streams. Household collection rounds include some trade clients. Street sweepings may be added to a trade or domestic round. Civic Amenity (CA) sites may mix trade and domestic waste. Few have their own weighbridges. Some streams unofficially switch into others. A major cause of the large rises recorded in household waste since the introduction of the landfill tax in Britain has been the seepage of trade waste into street litter, estate paladins, CA sites, or into the household dustbin stream. Some waste avoids official disposal altogether by being dumped illegally.

As a result, waste data is notoriously unreliable. Waste managers and government planners have no firm knowledge of the absolute quantities of particular streams, let alone their composition. Some years ago the UK Government had to increase its estimate of municipal waste by a third. Waste Strategy 2000 (and the Environment Agency) continue to use mechanical waste composition analyses undertaken for dustbin waste in the early 1990s as a proxy for the composition of all municipal waste, and consequently underestimate the quantity of organic waste by some 4-6 million tonnes. Twenty-year strategies in Britain are being based on quantities measured as household waste going over a weighbridge – whatever their source. Producers required to fund recycling under the packaging regulations have been in continuous conflict with the Environment Agency over the quantities of packaging waste.

Recycling cannot operate in such informational darkness. It needs to know waste quantities and compositions from its various sources not just in aggregate but for different rounds, streets and even households. For planning it has to know about waste trends by stream and also be able to estimate its 'reserves' of resources – how much newsprint, or cardboard or clothing there is in any town or city. For operations it has to be able to monitor the impact of diversion and what material is not being captured. For charging, it has to know how much each household or trader or institution is producing, since the principle that the polluter pays depends in practice on knowing the quantities produced by each 'polluter'.

The new waste economy has therefore become a close tracker of quantities. Some can be estimated by the size of bin (regularly re-sampled), some by statistical analyses using postcode marketing data.[43] Some municipalities have introduced on-board weighing of individual containers and expanded the number of weighbridges. All of them aim to produce detailed, real time data to allow them to track and adjust their systems promptly.

(iii) an audit of the current waste system

One of the principles of intensive recycling is that it should transform a local authority's (or a firm's) waste system and not be treated as an add-on to existing waste management. Many of the savings of the recycling-led systems have come from persistently inefficient features of the mass waste system – for example, from the practice of adding on the handling of mini-waste streams (such as special collections) piecemeal, to the mass waste system; from the reduction in 'defects' (such as missed pick-ups), or from the introduction of new systems into areas where waste management has broken down (high rise estates, urban street litter, and the fly-tipping of bulky goods). The costs of intensive recycling can also be reduced if it calls on, or increases its use of, existing assets – the corner of a local depot, for instance, or a well maintained collection vehicle which is available on weekends. The devil of 'smart recycling' is in the detail.

An initial audit is a survey of this detail. It will include:

- the assets held by the existing waste departments (lorries, depots, workshops, bulking bays, containers, databases, landfills) and by other waste generating/waste managing departments (notably housing, education, parks and highways). Most housing estates, for example, have unused collective areas – empty shops or garages that can be used as mini recycling depots. Parks have space and machinery suitable for composting. Highways have specialist vehicles and depots that could be rented for recycling;

- the operating patterns, schedules, capacity utilisation, breakdowns, distance to disposal and maintenance arrangements;

- the costs and income not just of the waste departments, but of all sections of the authority producing waste (one study in a London borough found that the per tonne cost of waste management on estates was nearly ten times that for ordinary domestic refuse rounds). Authority-wide costing will be the base marker or bottom line against which the costs of any new waste system have to be judged.

6. Social marketing

Earlier I discussed the central place of environmental values in the design and operation of successful recycling schemes. However, no service of this kind can succeed on ethics alone. The experience of both environmental and ethical trading is that the qualities normally expected of a service or commodity are the primary issue. Ethical market research shows that there are a small minority (often no more than 1%) who will buy recycled paper or fairly traded coffee whatever the quality. A further 30% are actively sympathetic to the ideas in question, and may even be willing to pay a little more (say an extra 10%) if the item in question is equivalent to conventional goods in quality. Another 40% will buy if both price and quality match the competition. A residual cohort remain indifferent or are even hostile. These proportions can change over time but the principle of an ethical 'bell curve' still holds.

Recycling has learnt similar lessons. For most people, the environmental value of the service is not enough if the service is irregular or inconvenient. To achieve high levels of participation recyclers have had to ensure that, in addition to the focus on 'meaning', they also offer a high quality service and employ the skills and social marketing techniques required. If recycling is in competition with the dustbin, then it has to be organised in a way that maximises its advantages and minimises its drawbacks. Among the points of importance are the following:

- *simplicity.* The highest participation rates come from a weekly service, preferably on the same day as a residual collection;

- *convenience.* Recycling boxes and organic containers need to be designed to take account first and foremost of householder convenience, with vertical boxes for flats for example, or small 'compostainers' for collecting organics in the sink;

- *design.* Good services require good design – of equipment, containers, workwear, and leaflets;

- *advice.* If householders are producers, then some aspects of recycling require advice. In the case of composting, the best schemes have employed compost doctors to help establish a compost bin, and to troubleshoot for those with problems; for recycling the collector can usually advise on materials that should be left out or included;

- *tracking.* Bar codes on recycling boxes have allowed collectors to monitor participation rates, with thanks to those who participate regularly, and direct approaches to those who don't;

- *feedback.* Regular feedback on the quantities of material collected and its use has been found to increase participation rates. This can be done through a newsletter left in the recycling box (boxes are now available with message slots so that they become a weekly vehicle for communication);

- *support groups*. Many recycling programmes have been organised with a supporters network, which acts as a point of advocacy and feedback from the street. Its views, along with those of the collectors and the customary focus groups, are important in assessing and expanding the service.

These approaches take one beyond a common view that only a minority of the population will engage in recycling, and that the issue is one of educating an ill-informed public. There are issues of information and education, but the lessons of environmental and ethical business are that a service like recycling must always present itself as both householder-friendly and a bearer of meaning. Like Oliver Cromwell, it must trust in God and keep its powder dry.

7. User pay and paying the user

The substance and quality of a service is more important for many householders than the relative 'effort price' of recycling. Yet many of the high performing programmes internationally have introduced user pay systems ('pay as you throw') for residual waste and/or some form of compulsory regulation. The advice of programme designers is to ensure that convenient systems are in place before introducing user pay or prohibitions, since it will otherwise lead to increased fly-tipping or free loading on others. Carefully introduced user pay (whether or not supported by regulation) shifts the form of payment for waste from a lump sum tax charge to a per-unit fee, and increases participation and capture rates by 10-15%.

There are some restrictions on the introduction of user charges in the UK, since local authorities are required under the Environmental Protection Act of 1990 to provide a free waste collection service. Paradoxically, this encourages a broader view of incentives than a simple mixed-waste user fee.

There are a number of ways in which a local authority in the UK can change the 'price' of recycling relative to the residual dustbin, in addition to the aspects of service quality outlined above. It can:

- charge for the provision of sacks or other containers (thus some authorities make a charge for plastic sacks for residual waste, but provide recycling and composting containers free. In North America householders are often charged different annual rates according to the residual bin size that they agree to use – a similar effect can be achieved by using the instruments legally open to local authorities in the UK);

- charge for collecting green waste and bulky goods;

- raise the level of annual charge for waste services and provide discounts for those households which join a recycling scheme (the discounts can be financial or in kind – a pilot of this kind is currently underway in the London Borough of Brent);

- introduce the Australian tag bag system and organise a prize draw for recycling. Each recycling bag is secure with a tag that carries a bar code on it. There is a weekly draw, the winner's bag is then checked, and if it is properly sorted, he or she receives substantial prizes – holidays to the Caribbean, a new low-emission car and so on. The savings resulting from introducing the scheme are shared with householders in this way;

- other forms of incentives along similar lines include free or subsidised goods and services for regular recyclers (water butts or extra composters for example, compost that can be collected free on certain days of the year, free energy saving advice, access to discounts on environmentally friendly goods negotiated on a bulk basis by the local authority, street/estate/village awards for good recyclers);

- many authorities in the UK and continental Europe have introduced town cards that act as a tool for providing resident discounts and for promoting public facilities and/or local and less recognised goods and services. Recycling and composting can easily be added to such 'smart cards', giving waste managers the flexibility of awarding bonus points and special offers to encourage participation;

- incentives of this kind can be used not simply to promote recycling in general, but to support particular 'campaigns' through 'targeted incentives' just as a firm would do when launching a new product;

One striking example of the incentive approach was introduced by the Mayor of Curatiba in Brazil. Faced with a crisis in waste collection, the municipality offered to pay residents for their waste if it was delivered to a local collection point. This generated an informal economy of collection, with low-income groups offering to take other people's waste so that they could collect the municipal payment. In effect it was a funded bring system – and in Curatiba's case part of the payment was made in food tokens which could be used to purchase the produce of local farmers. Bottle deposit schemes are another example of 'paying the user' rather than 'user pay', but the idea could be extended for particular materials such as aluminium (cans or foil), or – with expanded producer responsibility – for returnable consumer durables, in each case the price paid being covered by savings in collection costs.

In addition to flexible price and bonus schemes of this kind, the same goals can be approached using regulations and relative service differentials. A local authority in the UK has a variety of ways of strengthening recycling relative to the residual dustbin. Even with current legislation it can:

- require householders to use particular types of container (such as a blue box for recyclables or a plastic bin for food waste);

- limit the size of the permitted residual container if

other recycling containers are provided;

- refuse to pick up waste that is not properly sorted (this has been important to the success of the organic scheme in Bury St Edmunds; the collectors explain that they will not pick up organic bins contaminated with non-organics and this has led to a rapidly improved quality of set-outs);

- schedule waste collections that are more regular for recycling than residuals (a fortnightly collection of residuals and careful monitoring of dry recyclable and organic put-outs will encourage householders to recycle).

In some North American schemes, regulations are enforced by 'recycling police' who inspect dustbins in order to enforce bans and separation orders. For highly toxic materials, bans are important, but the lesson from successful programmes overseas is that the carrot of incentives and the imaginative use of social marketing are as important as the stick of controls.

8. Material marketing

Recycling in its initial stages is supply-led. It is an alternative way of dealing with waste, and provides materials for which, in some cases, there is no ready domestic demand. In the early 1990s on the West Coast of the USA, plastics piled up in warehouses and were eventually shipped to China. Germany found its supply of old newspapers outstripped the capacity of local reprocessing mills. The separate organic collections introduced in the Netherlands in the mid-1990s led to a surplus of compost, and so on. The story is a common one in the early period of expanded recycling and is particularly daunting for those in municipal recycling facing the market for the first time.

There are three points to keep in mind. First, imbalances of supply and demand are the norm in areas of new growth. This is the way the market works. Planners in the past have tried to limit these imbalances by ensuring that demand expanded in tandem with supply (it was referred to as balanced growth). But other economists (who favoured unbalanced growth) pointed out that these balances were difficult to gauge and that imbalances provided signals for innovation and expansion in unforeseen areas.

This has certainly been the case with recycling: the initial over-supply of recyclate, which resulted in unsustainable exporting or downcycling, nevertheless provided a secure source of material which prompted industries to convert to recycled inputs. The newsprint mills in North America, for example, took five to ten years to realise that recycled newsprint was the area for future growth. De-inking technology developed, and now it is the recycled mills that are earning the returns on Wall Street. The growth of demand for plastics, tyres and glass has followed a similar pattern.

Market development institutions like the Clean Washington Centre, The Materials for the Future Foundation in San Francisco and The Recovered Materials Foundation in Christchurch New Zealand, hasten the transition. Latecomers to recycling can also sell on the growing international market for recyclates. As a general proposition, the supply of recyclate creates its own demand. The initial depression of prices should be treated as a start-up cost and an issue of investment finances rather than an inherent limitation of intensive recycling.

Second, there is an issue of quality. In spite of its supply-driven origins, recycling needs to be designed and managed in relation to demand. In some cases that demand will need to be developed, but in others it is already there and the critical issue is quality. Paper that arrives wet and contaminated at a mill will be rejected. Glass bottle recycling is sensitive to stone and colour contamination. Tin cans recovered after incineration are degraded. In other words, the issue of markets and price is not just a question of external demand but of the quality of supply.

Recyclers should not see the market as a quasi-dustbin for offloading recyclates already collected. They have to be like any other supplier – attentive to quality, to delivery and to the requirements of the market. A good example is compost. The best compost programmes have been market-led. There are a wide variety of compost products, each with a different formula and requiring particular inputs. A good organics scheme should be able to supply composters with the requisite mix and without contamination. Where the supply of compost exceeds market demand, the need to restore soils means that there is still a use. Yet using compost for regenerating agricultural soils makes equal demands on the compost makers with respect to quality, standards and so on. The most common problem with compost is that its level of contamination is such that it is unfit to re-enter the biological cycle.

In these examples, what appears as a problem of markets is in fact a displaced problem of production. Even when local markets are slow to develop, there will always be outlets for good quality products. The only issue is price.

As a general rule, recycling programmes have experienced a secular increase in the level of material prices. For instance, a package of household recyclables in Canada, which in 1990 was worth on average £10-£15 a tonne, has now risen to some £40 a tonne.

There are four reasons for this type of effect:

- new investment that is made in response to cheap secondary materials prices expands demand, thereby pulling up the price;

- the development of new uses of secondary materials (up-cycling), such as glass as a filtration medium, can yield higher prices than feeding the materials back into their original use;

- improved quality should be reflected in higher prices;

- recyclers have found ways of reducing their dependence on the monopoly purchasers who dominate many of the secondary materials markets. In the short run, recyclers have formed supply consortia to improve their market knowledge and bargaining power. Such consortia have also been able to make arrangements for alternative outlets (export markets for paper and glass for example) and to reduce the impact of price fluctuations by negotiating long-term supply contracts at guaranteed prices.

The overall conclusion is that successful recyclers have been market makers as much as market takers. They see material markets not as a barrier but as a competitive space which demands sales expertise and the idea of the 'product as service'.

9. Disposal

Policies for Zero Waste need a strategy for the disposal of the residual waste that is integrated with the expansion of recycling. There are six principles of importance:

- *rapid diversion.* Recycling and composting should be expanded as quickly as possible in order to conserve existing disposal capacity;

- *cleaning the residual.* Priority should be given to the removal from the residual of those substances that are harmful in landfills, notably biodegradables and hazardous materials;

- *pre-treating the residual.* Further sterilisation of the residual can be achieved through establishing modular mechanical biological treatment (MBT) plants (now widely used in Germany, Austria, Italy and Canada), that sort the remaining organics from the residual waste stream and compost them prior to landfill or digestion. These plants should be designed so that they can be converted to in-vessel composting units for separated organics as the residual stream is reduced.

- *waste analysis centres.* Residual wastes should be continuously monitored on their entry to landfills as a form of quality control and a means of assessing the progress of the policies of diversion;

- *flexible disposal options.* Disposal is the safety net under Zero Waste. As such it is subject to multiple uncertainties – of composition and mass and of quantities rising or falling. It is important that the means of disposal be flexible, capable of being rapidly brought on-line, or held in abeyance, with low capital costs;

- *landfill as warehouse.* Landfills should be designed so that they can be economically excavated as technology advances for the further extraction of materials, unless they have been primarily intended to reclaim land using low value inert materials. They can also be used as holding areas for inert materials in temporary oversupply, like green glass.

10. Finance

There are five main features of recycling finance:

(i) *start-up costs.* There are initial deficits in intensive recycling. At the margin, recycling costs money. Municipalities and firms will expand recycling up to a point where market income and avoided disposal costs equal the marginal cost of collection. To go beyond that, by introducing separate collections of organics or dry recyclables, will lead to extra budgetary expenditure. This sets up a budgetary block to transition;

(ii) *declining costs.* Initial recycling costs tend to be at least double those of traditional forms of waste disposal (between £110 and £150 per tonne according to studies of UK recycling pilots, compared to £50-£60 a tonne for traditional waste management). But these costs fall as participation and capture rates increase, and high value materials are targeted. In economic terms, recycling enjoys economies of scale (the more throughput the cheaper the unit cost), economies of scope (lower unit costs per material as higher quantities of different materials are collected), economies of density and economies of communication. The benchmark norm for established collecting and processing of dry recyclables is a gross cost of £70 a tonne;

(iii) *dual income streams.* There are two sources of long-term revenue: core budgetary funding and material income. As the latter rises, the former can reduce;

(iv) *investment in intangibles* rather than fixed assets;

(v) *long-term system viability.* As collection and processing costs fall, income rises and savings increase through reduced residual collections.

What this means is that intensive recycling has almost everywhere required initial finance to launch it. Among the range of sources are the following:

- capital grants or subsidised finance for initial investment;

- grants for intangibles such as the development of information systems, training, and social marketing;

- revenue guarantees for material income;

- operating cost sharing;

- Producer Responsibility payments (as with the Green Dot scheme in Germany and the industry stewardship agreements in Canada);

- transfers of savings in disposal costs (as in the UK

recycling credit schemes);

- hypothecated taxes or charges.

This finance has been aimed at two things. First, the incremental transition costs of running multi-stream systems and second, risk management instruments to provide municipalities with income security. In general, systems costs savings have been most readily made when there is unified management of all collection (since this allows the extra costs of separate collections to be partially offset by savings on residual rounds), and when there are means for recyclers to capture the savings in disposal.[44]

Conclusion

Recycling and composting are now taking off in an increasing number of places. The turning point comes when diversion reaches 50% and becomes the principal form of waste management. Those involved by then have confidence in the practicality of recycling. Through experience they have an understanding of the alternative paradigm which has brought them this far and will take them further.

The leading authorities are committed to further expansion. They do not recognise a limit beyond which recycling cannot go. Latecomers have seen this and are setting more demanding targets. Toronto, with a current level of only 24% diversion, has just finalised its plans to achieve 60% by 2006 and Zero Waste by 2010. The leading recycling municipalities now see Zero Waste as a realisable target and no longer just a slogan.

They will not realise it alone. There needs to be change at the front end of production to match the advance at the back end. There are some materials – notably plastics – which have an unsustainably high recycling cost (over £300 a tonne in the case of one Canadian study of plastic bottles, more than ten times the cost of collecting mixed waste), just as there are products which are difficult to recycle. The main drivers in waste reduction will be designers and producers rather than the discard collectors. Fortunately these changes are already in train. Major innovations are taking place in the industrial sector that run parallel to the expansion of recycling. They provide the second route to Zero Waste.

V The Green Materials Revolution

The transformations of the waste industry, though remarkable, are in many ways subordinate to the changes taking place in the field of materials. Like 'smart' recycling they reflect a change in the industrial paradigm.

Every long wave of industrial development, driven by a leading new technology, brings with it its own innovation in materials. Cotton, iron, steel, oil-based plastics and chemicals were the leading materials of previous long waves. The current fifth wave – centred on electronics – is marked not so much by a new material (although modern materials can now be composited for particular uses to an unprecedented extent) as by the pressure to reduce materials and their toxicity.

We live in an age – as far as materials are concerned – that strives for absence. It speaks of 'de-materialisation', of finding ways of avoiding production, of making more with less. Instead of labour productivity, its attention is turned to material productivity as a new frontier of innovation. Its interest is in 'clean production' rather than more production, in quality not quantity. The economy of space (reducing material extraction, minimising transport and cutting environmental pollution) is at long last emerging as a challenge to the long ascendancy of the economy of time.

What we can now see, with hindsight, is that the old mass production model which reached its social and economic limits in the late 1960s and early 1970s was also having problems with its material limits. The volume of industrial minerals, metals, non-renewable organics and agricultural and forestry products in the USA had doubled to 600 million tonnes p.a. between 1945 and 1970. It continued to grow. By 1995 it had risen by nearly as much again,[45] but by then the twin 'thunderclap' of Rachel Carson's Silent Spring and the Club of Rome's 'Limits to Growth', and all that followed from them, had been heard and internalised.

The controversies about waste and what to do about it should be seen in this context. Waste was one of the most tangible symptoms of the material excesses of mass production. Its volumes climbed with growth. The rising resistance to its disposal was one expression of the limit to the old industrial order and contributed to the elaboration of the alternative. Waste reduction is part of the new paradigm now being put into place.

From the time of the Rio Earth Summit in 1992, the full extent to which the environment is bearing on the direction of industrial development is becoming clear. Initially it was particular industries that most felt the pressure of the environmental critique – agriculture, chemicals, energy, oil and mining – and the industries reacted with defensive hostility. But post-Rio, leading corporations have come to recognise that the environment is a more general issue, and that environmental policy propositions can no longer be resisted in particularistic ways. Climate change, the depletion of the ozone layer and accumulating toxicity in land and sea have multiple sources and universal effects.

Eco-efficiency

A significant development in this period has been the expansion of the World Business Council for Sustainable Development (WBCSD), a congress of multinationals which sought to develop a positive corporate view of the environment, 'by business for business'. In 1997 two of its leading members published a major statement arising from the WBCSD discussions, called 'Eco-Efficiency'. It opened with the following explanation of the term:

'Its essence ... is contained in seven simple guidelines:

- reduce the material intensity of goods and services

- reduce the energy intensity of goods and services

- reduce toxic dispersion

- enhance material recyclability

- maximise sustainable use of renewable resources

- extend product durability

- increase the service intensity of products

'Following these guidelines can give companies a competitive head-start into the next century – but not if they are treated as an add-on to "business as usual"... Eco-efficiency does require a profound change in their theory and practice of core business activities.'[46]

Like the early manifestos of Taylorism and Scientific Management, this sets out an entirely new way of thinking about production. The WBCSD has become a significant player in the movement to incorporate environmental issues within the industrial dynamic.

All seven of the above principles bear on the goals of Zero Waste. The reticence in the old waste industry to think in terms of Zero Waste is absent in the wider commercial world. 'Zero Waste' has become one of the watchwords of eco-efficiency. In the words of Edgar Woolard Jr, former chairman of DuPont, 'The goal is zero: zero accidents, zero waste, zero emissions.' As noted earlier, the language adopted and the approach is that of Japanese Total Quality Management extended to eco-efficient management.

Major companies have begun to adopt zero targets. Bell Canada, Kimberley Clark, Du Pont, Honda, Toyota, Hewlett Packard, the Ricoh Group and Interface Carpets are all aiming for Zero Waste. Xerox set the goal of 'waste-free products from waste-free factories' and has introduced targets for solid and hazardous waste reduction, air emissions, waste water discharges, low energy usage and the inclusion of 25% post-consumer recycled material in its parts and packaging. Increasing numbers of firms are adopting medium-term waste reduction targets of 50% or more – in parallel with the municipal sector. The eco-efficiency literature is full of examples of firms cutting waste and toxic emissions by orders of magnitude.[47]

Eco-efficiency and innovation

In its early phases of application, eco-efficiency is applied to on-site processes and later to products.[48] This has led to the criticism that eco-efficiency merely provides a 'greenwash' to the existing industrial system. Running a chlorine factory with fewer emissions cannot obscure the fact that chlorine-based products are major sources of pollution as they pass down the chain. Or to take a recent British example, one of the UK incinerators was recently awarded the ISO 1401 standard for environmental performance at the very time when it was mixing its highly dioxinated fly and bottom ash, storing it in the open air and allowing it to be used in urban domestic construction projects as a means of waste reduction.

Were eco-efficiency to remain limited in this way, the criticism would be well founded. Yet when a new way of looking at production and product design comes into play, with new touchstones and sensitivities, it is impossible to confine the approach to the role of propping up old production. For a fresh paradigm of this sort opens up whole unexplored territories for development – for technology, for products and for 'productive systems', similar in many ways to those created by electronics. As with electronics, the industrial firms that fail to respond to the new opportunities will be sidelined by the firms that do. By the end of the 1990s environmental performance had become recognised as a key element of the new competition.

Clean Production

Clean production is one way in which eco-efficiency has moved beyond the old. The WBCSD guideline 'reduce toxic dispersion' is the weakest formulation of the seven and reflects the vigour with which some branches of the chemical industry have defended their products in spite of their prevalent toxicity.[49] Yet the pressure to develop green chemicals and alternative non-toxic products has been intense and increasingly successful. Environmental pressure has forced the phasing out of toxic products such as DDT, leaded petrol, CFCs and halons, and the Stockholm Convention on Persistent Organic Pollutants will now target a further twelve organochlorines.

At the same time new products have been developed – as alternatives to banned and threatened substances (examples would be wet cleaning as an alternative to dry cleaning, plant-based inks and dyes, lead-free paint, as well as the remarkable rise of organic and till free agriculture). While the Stockholm Convention covers only twelve out of the 70,000 chemicals now in use, this should not diminish its importance. It lays down a marker for greener production. It shows a readiness to phase out toxic materials whatever their economic significance, and it means the eyes of the world now have the full range of chemicals in their sights.

The commodity-service economy

A second area that is being transformed is that of durable goods. In many of the durable sectors waste has been handled beneath the managerial radar line, since the cost of disposal has been minimal. The introduction of producer responsibility legislation, and demands for increased recycling and resource efficiency, are changing this. Firms are being forced to re-assess their products from the viewpoint of product life and recyclability. A new 'durable' industrial paradigm is emerging as a result, variously described as de-materialisation, the access economy, and the 'servicising' economy. Each of these formulations points to the increasing significance of knowledge-based services to modern production and the declining economic significance of material products.

One of those closest to these changes is Walter Stahel, of the Product Life Institute in Geneva. He and his colleagues outline a picture that is defined not only by absence and the avoidance of production, but also by a whole series of reversals. There is reverse logistics, reverse manufacturing and reverse retailing. There are also many other 're-' words – not only the three Rs (reduce, reuse and recycle), but repair, remanufacture, refine and so on. In this looking-glass economy it is as though all the established processes of production are being connected up to those same processes, going the other way.[50]

Walter Stahel identifies four strategic paths that are being pursued, each running alongside and reinforcing the others.

(i) *production avoidance.* His examples include ploughing at night, which reduces weeds and weeding, zero energy housing, and health maintenance organisations. There are many other spheres of the economy (such as transport, water and of course waste) where production can be avoided through smart systems. At the level of systems, this involves the redesign of 'productive systems' so that they require fewer material inputs to produce a desired outcome.

(ii) *extended product life.* This can be achieved by concentrating on another series of 're-s' – repair, re-manufacture, re-covering, refining and reuse. To facilitate these, increased product life needs to be incorporated in the initial design. For example the cost of repair can be lowered through the modularising of design and the automation of fault diagnostics. The modularising of components across products will help repair and remanufacture. In cases where product life is heavily influenced by changes in appearance (fashion) rather than functional operation, products can be designed to allow for skin changes or re-covering. Dynamic modularisation allows technical advances to be incorporated into a re-covered product.

Activities such as repair can be carried out by the user, but repair is most likely to be expanded if it is made the responsibility of the original producer. If a producer's goal is to extend product life (and the market should be shaped so that there is an incentive to do so), then we should expect there to be an increase in the leasing, rather than selling, of durable goods. Leasing would encourage long life design, and allow the manufacturer to plan the periodic activities such as maintenance, overhaul, re-skinning and so forth, that are necessary for continued product effectiveness. In the case of refining (of oils and solvents for example) renting the substances allows the manufacturer to remove the contaminants so that they can be reused.

(iii) *extended material life.* This is where recycling is relevant. In the case of end-of-life durable goods, recycling involves the reverse engineering of the assembly or flow processes by which they were produced. Industry symposia on the subject discuss such issues as the establishment of disassembly lines, new types of binders (such as glues and solders) that can be readily cracked open, and ways of decomposing composites or replacing them with recyclable materials. These processes are again often best undertaken by the original producers (using take-back, buy-back or leasing arrangements of the original commodities). They can then use more expensive but longer lasting materials (which would otherwise be lost to scrap) and 'learn from undoing' in order to revise product design to ease disassembly and recycling.

(iv) *increased product utilisation.* Many durable products are severely underused. One approach to increasing utilisation is through share schemes, like Lufthansa's car pool, or user friendly hire schemes. Another is through actual or de facto borrowing or leasing schemes. The disposable camera is one example; another would be the supply of equipment from a leasing company on request. These are all means of improving resource productivity, defined as an increase in outcomes per unit of material input.

The commodity-service economy

One of the results of these strategies is the emergence of a 'new service economy' in which manufacturers sell not commodities but service packages to achieve required outcomes. Manufacturing is transformed into a branch of the service sector, producing goods that are judged primarily on their performance as part of a service package.

In the case of energy, facilities managers offer target levels of power and comfort, and then employ an array of technologies in addition to (reduced) energy inputs in order to meet them. Rentokil offers pest control and security rather than rat poison and locks. Dupont is moving from supplying paint to the auto sector to supplying painted car bodies. Xerox supplies copying services. Fleet management offers mobility services for the transport of goods. As with leased buildings and elevators, such product + service provision is established and growing.

These examples largely come from the commercial sector, which is where the new commodity-service economy has first taken hold. It is now extending to consumer goods. Electrolux is supplying 'washing services' to households. Unilever has launched a cleaning service, which it hopes to extend into gardening services, providing the equipment and inputs in each case. A leading oil company is considering renting out oil as part of a lubrication service. Car companies are preparing to sell mobility services, with the consumer renting a given number of miles, supplied through a leased car, with insurance, fuel, maintenance and repairs provided.[51] In all these cases the commodity moves away from the centre of the commercial transaction and becomes what the industrial ecologists describe as 'a service delivery platform'.

One of the factors underlying this change is that so much consumption involves work. Cooking, washing, cleaning, gardening, house and car maintenance, travelling, shopping, child rearing, home caring and household information management are all part of the domestic economy. Toffler called it 'pro-sumption' and it now extends not just to the daily tasks but to self-education, to healthy living, and the management of a household's energy, water and waste.

The rise of commodity-plus-service reflects both changing work patterns and the application of modern technology in the home. Firms are now offering a 'three star' service package or a package of commodities, with guarantees and advice. In doing so they are changing their orientation, placing a premium on the continuing service-provider/customer relationship instead of the one-off commodity sale.

These changes place the responsibility (and risk) for product performance back with the manufacturer. As such they are parallel to the movement towards producer responsibility in waste. Taken together they enable issues of product and material life cycles to be re-integrated with the function of product design, opening out extraordinary opportunities for design innovation geared to increased material productivity and Zero Waste. For once the revenue of service providers is based on outcomes and they take responsibility for risk and waste, they have an interest in minimising both as well as the specialist capacity to do so.

The changes involved in such a shift are summarised in Table 2, drawing on the work of Walter Stahel and his colleagues.

Table 2
Characteristics of the new commodity-service economy

Commodity-based economy	Service based economy
Efficiency	Sufficiency
Output	Outcome
Vertical integration of producer and supplier	Vertical integration of producer and customer
Doing things right	Doing the right thing
Labour productivity	Resource productivity: resource input per unit of outcome produced
River economy (cradle to grave)	Lake economy (cradle to cradle)
Cost reduction production based asset management	Performance-management
Flow process and assembly	Disassembly and reverse manufacturing
Global factories	Local workshops
Commodity as inflexible mechanised service package	Commodity as service delivery platform
One-off sale	Long-term service contracts and guarantees/take-back and buy-back
Purchase	Lease
Risk borne by consumer (caveat emptor)	Risk borne by producer (caveat factor)
Individual consumption	Shared consumption

Product specific components components	Standardised
Product-based standards based standards	Performance-based standards
Private and public property and collective responsibility	Rights of access
Material and discard intensive	Zero Waste

The expansion of commodity-service

In 1999-2000 the Product Life Institute undertook a study of the significance of the new commodity-service economy. The results were the following. The EU market for products sold as services in 1998 was 10% of GDP, of which 6% was accounted for by selling the function of products (such as fleet management) and 4% by re-manufacturing (principally in the building and construction sector). The shift to services has gone further in the USA, with a share of products sold as services up to 15% of GDP, and the re-manufacturing of components worth an estimated $50 billion.

The survey of leading edge companies in this field, which was part of the study, reported that they expected to double or quadruple their share of revenue selling services instead of products by 2010. The report concludes:

'If the existing trend continues, we expect to see by 2010 a European economy with a technically and socially perfected material recycling system for waste, in competition with a perfected Japanese "inverse manufacturing" technology sold on a global level to companies that drive a "loop economy" e.g. a multiple reuse of upgradable components and products in a system context; and many US companies selling performance instead of goods on a global level, through a generalised fleet management approach for several product groups which enables them to reach down to the customer.'[52]

Designing for cycles

The trends identified by Walter Stahel apply not only to durable goods. The example of oil and solvents shows the way in which a non-durable good can be changed into a durable one – or, in the new vocabulary, how every commodity can become a 'delivery platform' capable of repeat services, just as materials can be reconceptualised as delivery platforms for a succession of functions.

But there are other cases where the design is geared to switching materials from the technical to the biological cycle. This is one of the aims of the movement to replace the hydrocarbon with the carbohydrate economy, by substituting renewable materials for non-renewable or hazardous ones. Whereas leading economies in the early nineteenth century used two tons of vegetables to one ton of minerals, by 1970 they were using six tons of minerals to one ton of vegetables. Now there are pressures to throw this trend into reverse. The rise of oil prices, the advances of biological sciences, and environmental regulation directed at the polluting effects of oil and mineral-based production are all making vegetable-based products more competitive.[53]

Ethanol production using specialist biomass is likely to have reached 5 billion gallons by the end of 2001, and 10 billion by 2004. Vegetable inks now account for 10% of all printing inks. Lubricants are being made from decomposable vegetable oil. Starch-based biodegradable plastics made from wheat, maize and potatoes are expected to expand rapidly in food packaging (and in the management of waste). The first commercial foams made from soy oil are now appearing on the market.

Because packaging has been one of the first sectors to be covered by producer responsibility, accounting for more than a fifth of domestic dustbin waste, it has been the subject of a wave of innovations, many of them aimed at increasing its compostability. In addition to the starch-based plastic bags, the most recent innovation has been in the use of biodegradable calcium carbonate (chalk) combined with potato starch to produce disposable food packaging (including food boxes for McDonalds). A variant using calcium carbonate with a natural gas-derived plastic has been launched by the former owner of Tetra-Pak, to cut energy in production and reduce waste.[54]

Conclusion

The movement for eco-efficiency began as a managerial tool for environmental improvement. What transpires from the many eco-efficiency initiatives during the 1990s is that examining production from the perspective of materials, waste and hazards rather than simply flow, cost and time provides a stimulus to innovation which may also improve flow, save cost and cut time. Certainly, once external pressures force firms to look at their operations from a Zero Waste/zero emissions perspective, the rate of return on the time and investments involved can be remarkably high.

The eco-efficiency drive has also led to inter-firm collaboration, where the wastes of one producer become the inputs of another (in some instances centred in and around ecology parks) and to the creation of a demand for environmental advisory services and equipment. Eco-efficiency requires its own environmental managers, engineers, auditors and capital goods sector which together constitute a new industry.

The impact, however, has gone much wider than this – to the redesign of materials, products and whole processes of production. The purpose of these many new developments is not confined to waste, but they have major implications for it. Not only are they already creating a means of reducing waste, they are facilitating the way that discards can be reintroduced to material cycles. With some 70% of dustbin waste already being biodegradable, the gradual replacement of glass, metals and plastics by vegetable and chalk-based materials will give a further impetus to composting as a means of recycling waste.

Eco-design, clean chemicals and other aspects of the new biological and material sciences are set to transform the nature and quantity of waste over the next two decades. Factor Four and Factor Ten may underestimate the extent of the gains that will be made. One application of enzyme technology, for example, has allowed milk-whey waste to be used as a fuel, with a Factor 37,000 gain. Leading firms are integrating Zero Waste into the core of the industrial dynamic and moving rapidly up the Zero Waste mountain from the other side.

VI The Transition to Zero Waste

There is no longer any dispute about the need for a new waste order and for industrial processes that radically cut down on their use of fossil fuels and non-renewable resources. The pressures for change are persistent and accumulative. Nor is the feasibility of the alternative any more in question. For anyone doubting the reality of intensive recycling, examples in practice are only a plane trip away. Similarly Factor Four innovation and the new commodity-service economy are no longer subjects for Tomorrow's World. Many of them are already available.

Yet it is one thing to show the technical and economic feasibility of a new way of doing things. It is another to diffuse it beyond the pathbreakers. Those from an old industry commonly cannot conceive how their work could be organised in a different way. The process would not work; it is dangerous and too expensive; consumers wouldn't want it.[55] These interests usually have economic power and political influence derived from the old order. The inherited infrastructure reflects past needs, as does the balance of skills and organisational structures. As a result the advance from one paradigm to another has in the past taken place at the margins, where the old order is weaker.

One type of transition has depended on industrial pioneers who have developed the alternative in the face of such barriers, with market processes then diffusing the successful innovation, and the regulatory regime within which the industry operates being revised to take account of the innovation. In such market-led restructuring, interests seeking to defend old forms of production, even when they have political support, have been brought to heel by the market.

In the last thirty years a new type of environment-led industrial transition has emerged with a different dynamic. The primary innovators have been environmental and consumer movements. They have had some direct influence on the market, through 'green consumption' and ethical investment. But the key channel for change has come when the demands of these movements are translated into government policy and from there into the economy. A new fiscal and regulatory regime is necessary for the environmental economic dynamic to move from the margin to the mainstream. 'Green restructuring' is a politics-led not market-led process, even if it is carried through by a market that has been reshaped by economic instruments and regulations.

In any jurisdiction the tipping point comes when governments signal their intention to introduce new measures reflecting environmental goals. Political statements of intent are an invitation to industry to develop strategies and technologies that reflect these goals. It is then that the dynamic switches to the corporate sector. The new publicly signalled direction means that environmental performance becomes a central determinant of competitivity.

The above applies directly to the waste industry. In all OECD countries environmental movements have played a pioneering role, highlighting the hazards of landfills and incinerators, and proposing a recycling-intensive alternative. In many areas, activists started their own recycling and composting schemes. They have also proposed an alternative regulatory regime. As we can now see from a decade of experience elsewhere, the issue is not the practicality of the Zero Waste option. It is rather the readiness of government to introduce the regulations and price adjustments that will allow this to happen. Contrary to neo-liberal models of the economy, the direction of development in environmental industries such as waste will be determined by the government and the institutional and fiscal framework it sets for the market. It is not a question of government versus the market. The market can only operate within publicly established parameters. The two are complementary not alternative.

What I argue here is that new regulatory regimes for waste are emerging, with Europe now in the lead, which run parallel to increasingly far reaching international environmental agreements. Along with continued pressure from environmental and consumer movements, and the growing recognition of the environmental issues lying behind the agreements, these new public policy directions have led to an autonomous dynamic developing within the market economy. Year by year we can see that the world of waste and materials is moving from an era of pilots and prototypes into one of generalised innovation and diffusion.

A new regulatory regime

In the late 1980s it was not clear in any country whether or how a major shift from disposal to recycling would take place in the waste sector. Public opposition to landfill and incineration had emerged in North America and parts of continental Europe, but the stage of new government regulations had only begun to be reached.[56]

The key date, as with so many other events in East and West, was 1989. This was the year of the EU's Incineration Diretives followed two years later by the revised Waste Framework and Hazardous Waste Directives, which together became the marker for pollution control in Europe. From then on many European countries began to introduce their own laws and policies promoting recycling. Austria introduced its radical Waste Management Act (whose objectives mirror those of the Zero Waste option outlined above) in 1990, at the same time as the introduction of Switzerland's order banning the landfill of unsorted waste by 2000, as well as its beverage container order. Germany passed its packaging law in 1991. In North America the Californian recycling law was introduced in 1989. Seattle adopted its intensive recycling policy in that year. Shortly afterwards, Canada set 50% targets for all states by 2000.

Viewed historically, these were the years when policy opened up. In the USA shortages of landfill space and the difficulty in siting new landfills led to policies to promote incineration. In 1990 the US Environmental Protection Agency forecast that the proportion of waste incinerated in the USA would rise from 8% to 26% in 2000. Yet the degree of public opposition and the rising cost of incineration relative to landfill and recycling has meant the plans have largely been abandoned. During the 1980s and 1990s more than 300 incinerator proposals were halted through local opposition. After a brief expansion in the early 1990s, the number of plants fell from 170 in 1992 to 132 in 2000, and incineration's share of disposal is now back to 7%.

In Europe, Germany was likewise faced with landfill shortages and adopted a plan to build 120 incinerators. Strongly opposed by the Greens, the government managed only two dozen by the end of the 1990s, with many Länder abandoning incineration and turning to intensive recycling instead. The coming into force of the EU's tighter incineration standards led to widespread closures of incinerators and the costly upgrading of those that remained.

For landfill-oriented countries, the scope for an incinerator-led strategy was limited. Instead they turned to intensive recycling. The initial waste diversion legislation of the late 1980s and early 1990s was followed by a succession of national laws and ordinances promoting the new policies. Germany passed a 1994 Product Recycling and Waste Management Act, which focused on minimising the use of products that cannot be recycled or reused and on maximising recycling. This was followed by the 1996 'Closed Loop Economy Act' which sought to consolidate the industrial opportunities opened up by recycling. Austria introduced two ordinances on packaging (1993 and 1996) and on the collection of biogenic waste.

A second group of countries (the Netherlands, Denmark, Switzerland, Sweden and France) had a large numbers of incinerators, principally because of the difficulties of landfill. Landfill accounted for 13% or less of municipal waste tonnages in the Netherlands, Denmark and Switzerland. In these cases, the impetus to change came not so much from landfill shortages as from concern about the hazards of incineration.[57]

From the start of the 1990s, these countries followed a policy of closing or upgrading their incinerators and promoting the kind of recycling that did not undercut the incinerators' needs. Switzerland introduced user pay and producer responsibility legislation in 1995. Denmark implemented policies on the take-back of glass bottles and on construction and demolition waste, and approved an incinerator tax to aid recycling. The Netherlands passed a law in 1994 requiring all municipalities to organise separate organic collections, removing a low calorific material out of the waste stream.[58]

The 1990s, then, was the time for the spread of new environmental waste legislation. In Europe the lead was taken by a number of northern countries. The legislative innovations were then taken up and generalised in an amended form by the European Union.

The thrust of European policy has been in line with Zero Waste. It has had two elements. First the Commission has further tightened the performance standards required of landfill (in the Landfill Directive 1999) and incineration (2001) and is now preparing legislation that ensures that the liability for pollution resulting from disposal facilities is taken by the operators.

Second, it has promoted a shift towards producer responsibility and recycling through the Packaging Directive, the Waste Electrical and Electronic Goods Directive, and the End of Life Vehicle Directive. A Bio Waste Directive is being prepared and a recycling Directive is promised.[59] There is also the prospect of a further extension of the radical producer responsibility Directives, covering other products (such as batteries) and particular materials, like plastics. The latest EU policy signals a shift in emphasis from pollution control to the sustainable use of resources.[60]

These measures set in place a new waste regulatory regime. It has six features:

- strengthening pollution control of waste disposal – both of landfills and incinerators – as well as some forms of composting and recycling, and ensuring that the operators bear responsibility for any resulting pollution;

- a revised fiscal and regulatory regime that reflects the waste hierarchy: taxes, subsidies and regulations are being structured to reflect the generic waste hierarchy (reduction/reuse/recycling/recovery/landfill) and sub-hierarchies within each;

- producer and consumer responsibility: there is an emerging shift of financial responsibility for municipal waste disposal and diversion from the state to producers and consumers (shown in the extension of producer responsibility measures and in systems of 'user pay');

- from mass to niche waste: rather than a general regulatory structure for mixed waste, sub-regimes are emerging for particular types of waste, such as special and hazardous waste, organic and biodegradable wastes, and particular production chains and materials;

- multiple criteria underlying waste policy: traditionally pollution control and local health impacts have been the dominant criteria, but now the impacts of waste management methods on greenhouse gases, soil depletion, and the use of non-renewable resources are taken into account;

- proximity principle: the promotion of local disposal and recycling of waste, as a form of 'community responsibility'. This entails limiting international trade (including internal trade) in waste, and measures against waste dumping.[61]

What is striking about this process is that Europe is now able to gain some of the flexibility of federal states such as

Canada, the USA and Australia. New policies are developed at a regional and national level. They are then diffused through European legislation, but are implemented back through the national governments. This is an open structure, which allows for variety and innovation within an overall strategic framework.

The economic dynamic

The movement to cleaner production and resource economy in the industrial sector has been a response less to this new waste regulatory order, than to the anti-pollution campaigns and regulations introduced over the past thirty years. These have prompted innovations in products and processes and provided much of the impetus behind the $50 billion worth of green industry technology that now exists worldwide. The regulations were directed at particular pollutants (such as lead and CFCs) or at media (clean air and clean water), processes (through improved scrubbing technology) or products (such as numerous pesticides).

Suppliers of the 'cleaner' technologies led the revolution. Many of the large corporations were more defensive, phasing out some products, substituting others, but for the most part continuing their trajectories of growth. The chlorine industry, for example, lost much of its gasoline-additive and pesticide business in the 1980s but recovered in the 1990s through the promotion of PVC plastic.

In the past decade, however, the impact of the resource revolution has widened, and it has developed its own market momentum. In the business sector, the implications (and potential) of the central environmental issues are no longer solely the focus of pioneers of green production and those sectors and places most subject to the force of environmental politics. They are being recognised now in terms of new areas of profitability and a new scale of risk.

One risk is climatic. The cost of natural disasters is forecast to rise to $53 trillion by 2050 primarily as a result of global warming. That cost will have to be covered – at least in part – by the corporate sector. Another risk is the threat of market collapse, where materials or products prove to be hazardous, and lead to compensation claims against their producers. A third is the effect of environmental and consumer 'buy-cotts' and campaigns centred on firms in contentious industries (from oil to life sciences).

All these are forcing a change in the level of corporate response. A window onto this change is provided by the shifting role of corporate environmental managers. In little more than a decade they have seen their job descriptions expand from responding to particular issues (such as pollution incidents or the threat of legislation) to the promotion of cost-reducing eco-efficiency initiatives, to audits and systems design within the context of total quality management, and most recently to the much wider strategic issues of assessing whole production systems against the criteria of 'sustainable development'.[62]

Firms are recognising that they can no longer consider environmental issues simply as external 'threats' or even as prompts to operational best practice, but must consider wider systemic questions. Those that do not respond are now under pressure – from institutional and other shareholders as well as from new entrants. The issue of environmental risk and how it is managed has now entered the corporate bottom line.[63]

The insurance industry is an important source of pressure. It is at the centre of the new 'risk economy'. Without major changes in the way the economy is run, it faces levels of claim which threaten its future and the very concept of insurability. Insurers are now using their market power – through fund managing intermediaries – to make corporations accountable for their environmental practices. In early 2001, for example, Morley Fund Management, a leading UK fund manager owned by the largest UK insurer, CGNU, and managing £100 billion worth of assets – equivalent to 2.5% of the UK stock market – announced that it will vote against the annual accounts of any of the top 100 companies which does not file an environmental report (only 37 currently do so), and abstain on those in the top 250 which are in high risk sectors (including oil and gas, electricity, chemicals, automobiles and construction).[64]

A parallel pressure comes from the pension funds, which are required under recent UK law to disclose in their annual accounts whether they are taking environmental, ethical and social considerations into account in making their long-term investments. They, too, are pressing fund managers to focus on the 'green bottom line' through the use of vetoes at annual shareholder meetings and direct negotiation.

Conclusion

The regulatory and economic dynamics are increasingly marching in step. Producer responsibility initiatives take the process further. Packaging is already being transformed by the impact of regulations. The trends evident in the consumer durable sectors will be spread further by the new EU Directives on electrical and electronic goods and end-of-life vehicles. Those firms considering their ten- and twenty-year strategies can see more clearly the shape of the landscape ahead and are making their plans accordingly.

VII Re-orienting UK waste

The political 'crisis of transition' has come later in Britain than it has in much of Europe and North America. Until the late 1990s waste was not a national political issue. Britain's geology and widespread mineral production allowed a continual replenishment of landfill space. When incinerator capacity contracted in the mid-1990s, landfill was available to take up the slack. There was some local opposition to new landfills, but this was fragmented and lacked a national presence. The environmental movement focussed on other issues such as road building and food, and was in any case weakly represented in formal politics because of the first past the post voting system.

There was, as a result, no strong internal pressure for British waste policy to engage with the new resource economy. While other EU countries have been transforming waste into secondary materials at a level unmatched since the Second World War, Britain remains stuck in the bottom four of the EU municipal recycling league and is in danger of missing out on the economic potential of 'closed loop industrialisation'.

In 1990 the UK household recycling rate was an estimated 2.5%. In line with the turn towards recycling, the Government set a target rate of 25% by 2000. By the time of the next White Paper in December 1995 ("Making Waste Work") the rate was estimated at 5%. The White Paper was still confident, however, that the 25% target could be achieved by 2000 and set a range of other targets for particular materials.

The results are now in for the target year 2000. Household recycling has risen to 10%, still at the foothills of the S curve, and less than a quarter of the rates of leading continental countries. Only Portugal, Greece and Ireland in the EU have lower figures than the UK. If Britain were an American state, it would find itself seventh from bottom of the interstate recycling league.

For individual materials the picture is similar. In the case of packaging materials – which had been targeted for recycling by many countries and by the EU – Britain still only recycled 27% from all sources in 1998 (bolstered by paper and cardboard from the commercial sector), way below most other European countries (see Tables 3-5). In 1998 the UK recycled 38% of its aluminium cans as against 89% in Switzerland, despite having the largest aluminium can recycling plant in Europe. By 1999 Britain was still only recapturing 25% of its glass containers compared to 93% in Switzerland, and 30% of its steel packaging as against 80% in Germany.

In the construction sector, the UK rate of recycling of 43% is less than half the 90% achieved in parts of Denmark and now adopted as a national target by 2005 in Holland. In newsprint, which has traditionally had higher rates of recycling, Britain is noted for having the largest untapped supplies of old newspapers of any country in Europe. Composting organic waste remains a marginal activity in both the commercial and household sectors, with only 80 centralised compost sites compared to more than 1,000 in

Table 3 European steel packaging recycling
Country Recycling rate 1999 (%)

Country	Rate
Germany	80
Netherlands	78
Austria	75
Belgium	70
Luxembourg	69
Switzerland	66
Sweden	62
Norway	59
France	47
Spain	32
UK	30

Source: APEAL in FoE 2001

Table 4 European aluminium can recycling
Country Recycling rate 1998 (%)

Switzerland	89
Sweden	87
Germany	86
Finland	84
Norway and Iceland	80
Benelux	66
Austria	50
UK	38
Spain	21
France	19

Source: European Aluminium Association in FoE 2001

Table 5 European container glass collection
Country Recycling rate 1999 (%)

Switzerland	93
Netherlands	86
Austria	84
Sweden	84
Norway	83
Germany	81*
Finland	78
Denmark	63
France	55
Portugal	42
Italy	41
Spain	40
Ireland	35
Greece	27*
UK	25

Source: FEVE in FoE 2001 *1998 figures

Zero Waste

Germany.[65] Only 8% of household organics in England and Wales was centrally composted in 1999/2000, principally garden waste taken to CA sites.

As a result of this poor recycling performance, the lead in developing new sorting and processing technologies has been taken by North American and continental European countries. Germany, Holland, Scandinavia, Canada and the USA dominate the international trade fairs in these fields. In the case of electrical and electronic goods, for example, the reluctance of the UK Government and UK firms to move on producer responsibility until the EU required them to do so means that other EU countries that introduced national legislation early have been given a ten-year start in developing the requisite technology. The same thing has happened in closed vessel composting, in the electronic sorting of plastic and paper, in the technology for recycling container glass and in a wide variety of new uses for recycled material that have been developed in North America.

On any count, British recycling policy is a case study in failure. The targets set for municipal recycling were half those of more ambitious jurisdictions, and only a third of the modest targeted increase was achieved. If a school or hospital had failed to reach its targets to this extent it would no doubt be subject to Special Measures. But in the case of waste, the Special Measures need to be applied to the government itself.

If things are to change, the starting point has to be a recognition of the reasons for failure, and the need for a quite different policy approach. It is not as though civil servants were unaware of the environmental advantages of recycling, or of the principal reasons why it has remained so little developed. In the second half of the 1990s there were numerous national and international studies on the subject, and on policies which had been successful in stimulating recycling elsewhere. The question is why so little came out of them, and why the international examples of successful recycling were read less as a guide to good practice than as exceptions that could not happen here.

The explanations of policy failures of this kind usually include failures of political will, the conservatism of the British civil service, and the power of threatened economic interests. In the case of waste, none of these is sufficient. The two environment ministers in the second half of the 1990s, one Conservative and one Labour, were both committed to increasing recycling and did what they could to advance it.[66] Many of the civil servants involved played a central part in one of the most radical periods of British government. And as for economic interests, the traditional waste industry does not have large numbers of sponsored MPs or an economic presence that carries weight in the calculus of politics.

Rather, two wider questions should be examined: the first is the type of policy and institution necessary for environmental transition; the second is the model of government that determined the way issues were approached during the 1990s.

(i) the process of transition

For a new waste order to become established, there must first be clear directives from government and/or incentives strong enough to force old institutions to change and attract new entrants to the industry. In the UK there has been neither. The non-mandatory targets set for household and commercial recycling during the 1990s were largely ignored, and the structure of incentives was such that it is surprising that recycling increased at all.

The economic point is the important one. The first and immediate reason why recycling targets have not been met is that those involved in the management of waste have had little incentive to promote them. In terms of the commercial market, as it is currently structured, only low level recycling can break even, and even then it lies at the bottom of the hierarchy of profitability. In the words of one financial analyst of the waste sector, "Recycling remains a commercial leper in the UK".[67] Since intensive recycling also demands a profound change in industrial organisation and methods as well as cutting into the industry's core business, it is a triply unattractive proposition to existing waste companies. Not surprisingly their focus has remained on mass waste collection and disposal.

From a municipal perspective, intensive recycling has been seen as prohibitively expensive by collection authorities and saves no money for disposal authorities, since the money saved by diverting waste from disposal has to be passed on to the collectors as recycling credits. Nor have disposal authorities welcomed a proposition that threatens to shift the axis of waste management from disposal to collection, and thus undermine their traditional function.

As a result, collection authorities have by and large restricted recycling to what can be afforded with a balanced or small incremental budget, using low cost methods of bring banks and/or periodic kerbside collections of the most marketable dry recyclables. Few have been able to afford three stream systems or provide the working capital necessary to benefit from the resulting 'system economies'. For the most part they remain caught in the low-level recycling trap.

Major waste companies and disposal authorities, for their part, have confined recycling to bring schemes at CA sites and to methods that fit in with the traditional way of doing things. They have not promoted recycling but have introduced it only when required to do so as part of a larger contract or in response to regulatory requirement. They favour capital-intensive sorting and composting plants, with limited source separation, and large collection vehicles. They have not invested in social marketing and frontline advisory services, nor in the management information systems required by 'smart' recycling systems. The result is relatively poor participation and capture rates and low levels of recycling. Organising recycling using the old methods has led them to see recycling as difficult, expensive and limited in what it can recover.

Although kerbside collection has expanded in the past five years, it still accounts for only 3% of household waste. The bulk (71%) of the household recycling that has taken place has relied on householders travelling to bring banks and CA sites.

The 1990s have seen substantial change in the waste industry: in the technology of landfills and incinerators; in the beginnings of new forms of pre-treatment of waste; and in the concentration of ownership in the industry. But the response to the new regulatory regime emerging from Brussels has been within the framework of the old waste paradigm. Thus the requirements of the Landfill Directive to divert biodegradable waste from landfill (65% of 1995 levels by 2020) have been primarily considered in terms of mixed waste treatment alternatives rather than the development of intensive source-separated recycling. The provision of capital intensive mixed waste treatment plants means that the forms of collection, compaction, transport, labour and contracting can be left largely unaltered. Change is confined to methods of disposal and their technologies. Administratively, the planning and organisation of waste disposal is able to continue as before.

This is why the new taxes, regulations and charges that lie behind the changes of the 1990s have been accepted without demur, even when in the case of disposal authorities, they have led to steeply increased costs. For the waste industry, disposal authorities, central Government and waste consultants, business has been able to continue as usual. Like Lampedusa's Prince, they have embraced change so that things can remain the same.

It is not that the waste industry or the waste profession will not take up recycling; rather that the returns must be such that it worth their while to restructure their assets and skills. Strikingly, one of the major UK waste firms has invested heavily and successfully in recycling and composting operations in Belgium and the Netherlands, where returns are high, while remaining oriented to disposal in the UK where the incentives are absent. Another of the waste majors has gone further, redefining its long run strategy as secondary resource management, but has been restricted by perverse waste markets and institutions from putting this into practice.

So a change in incentives is the first necessary condition for a transition to Zero Waste. To speed up the change it is also necessary to have transitional institutions, unencumbered by past interests and outlooks, to provide the knowledge and resources required by the new paradigm. Five types of institution have been important for the development of Zero Waste programmes elsewhere:

- those promoting new uses of secondary materials, and innovative market instruments;

- those supplying know-how in waste reduction and the establishment and operation of high capture/low cost recycling systems;

- those forming a new resource-oriented profession (such as training and management programmes, research centres and professional journals);

- champions of clean production and pollution control (through a network of testing centres, laboratories, research institutes and consultancies); and

- those providing transitional finance.

The first four of these are means of introducing the knowledge economy into traditional waste management, and until recently were either non-existent or ill developed in the UK. The fifth has taken a variety of forms overseas – direct grants, price supplements, investment finance – and is directed to provide start-up capital in a sector in which neither government departments nor private financial institutions have the instruments or knowledge to function effectively.

(ii) **light government**

The above list summarises the requirements for switching Britain from a waste disposal to a 'closed loop' resource economy. It poses a challenge to government, which during the 1990s was largely sidestepped. The reason was not to do with individuals but rather with a distinctly British approach to governance.

In the case of waste, there have been two forces shaping policy:

- the neo-liberal model of government that developed during the 1980s, which sought to reduce the role of the state and commercialise wherever possible the administration of government and public services;

- the trends in EU environmental policy that ran against such precepts by requiring more regulation, less trade and increased environmental taxes.

In the former, government took a back seat in determining how a sector developed; in the latter it became the driver. The tension between the 1980s model of government in Britain and that of 1990s Brussels – a tension which is still at the heart of British politics – is present also in the governance of waste.

The problem faced by the administrators was how to translate Brussels directives and their consequences into a neo-liberal framework. The result, as elaborated in successive white papers and policy guidances, had five features:

- *non-directive government.* The White Papers showed a reluctance to direct industry or local government as to the direction of their waste management. They set down criteria to inform those choices and established indicative parameters through non-mandatory targets. But the final 'mix' of waste management options was not to be determined from the centre. It would in any case vary with circumstance and should be judged against the principle of the Best Practical Environmental Option (BPEO).

- *marketisation*. All waste should be managed 'on a commercial and competitive basis', which meant enforcement of compulsory competitive tendering and the commercialisation/privatisation of local authority waste disposal operations. It also meant that those responsible for waste should have to pay for it ('the polluter pays'), substituting a market where possible for the tax/subsidy-based administration of household waste. The prices that ruled in such markets should, however, be adjusted to reflect the external costs and benefits of alternative means of waste management. This was the justification for the Non-Fossil Fuel Obligation (NFFO) as applied to energy from waste that ran from 1989, and for the landfill tax introduced in 1996. Where targets were compulsory as the result of EU Directives, quasi-markets were introduced to increase flexibility. The system of Packaging Recovery Notes gave 'obligated' firms a range of options in meeting their targets, and was seen as an instrument to achieve equilibrium between rising targets and the supply of recyclables. Similar proposals have been made for the trading of landfill permits.

- *private financing*. In parallel with this process of marketisation, direct government grant programmes were restricted. Instead the government used its fiscal and regulatory influence to re-route the flow of private funds. Thus in the case of waste, the NFFO was a charge paid by electricity supply firms to the operators of energy-from-waste (EfW) plants; the landfill tax credit scheme was a payment by landfill operators to environmental trusts; the Packaging Recovery Notes (PRN) system channelled money from the 'obligated parties' that produced and sold packaging to material reprocessors. These were innovative forms of finance, that effectively privatised the tax and spend function of government, subject to government guidelines. The expansion of the

Private Finance Initiative (PFI) in the late 1990s followed a similar principle with respect to the funding of public capital projects, although in the case of waste it needed substantial public subsidy to make it work.[68]

- *restricted regulation.* Regulations were limited to tightening the standards of landfill and incineration, and were not used to promote recycling or composting. The enforcement of regulation was centralised in the Environment Agency in 1996, as was the planning function for new waste facility proposals as they related to environment and health.

- *information.* Market models acknowledged that imperfect information could restrict the efficient working of markets (and the operability of targets). The government therefore undertook to promote the ideas of waste minimisation and improve data on waste arisings and composition as well as diffusing information and advice about waste minimisation in the industrial and commercial sectors.

The most interesting part of this approach in practice is how it handles those areas of policy where there are state requirements – principally as the result of European Directives. In the case of pollution control, regulatory regimes were established in close consultation with industry. They left scope for a considerable degree of self-inspection under a generalised duty of care. The Environment Agency, as the guardian of environmental health on behalf of the government, has interpreted its role as a narrow enforcer of regulations rather than a pro-active promoter of good environmental practice.[69]

Where the Directives set compulsory targets (as with the Packaging Regulations and the Landfill Directive), their application in the British context was put out to extensive consultation, and trading mechanisms proposed which increased the flexibility of those subject to the targets. In this way, the market was introduced into the process of target enforcement.

The important point to note is that while the EU issued Directives, the UK Government acted as a diffuser of direction. It neither wanted to, nor did it, take the lead. The 1995 White Paper, 'Making Waste Work', was explicit in saying that leadership in waste policy should be provided by the market and not by the government.

The principal role for the government was to establish the means of decentralising how waste is managed and financed, and how resources are distributed. Decisions about direction and operations were to be left to the market or the agencies, within guidelines and parameters established at the centre. It was and is a subaltern model of government.

The limits of light government

The British failure in recycling has highlighted four major flaws in this model of government. First, at a time when there were clear signals that the old waste order could no longer continue, the lack of government leadership on a new direction and of an explicit government goal for waste, left those involved in the old waste industry, as well as others who might participate in the new one, unclear about the future course of government policy in a sector whose direction is determined by government. The market cannot lead in the environmental field when the parameters within which the market works are set by government fiscal and regulatory policy. The market has to be 'made' before it can be a maker, particularly in an area like waste, which requires the industry to change so radically, and new types of industry to emerge. Neither established firms nor new entrants are likely to invest heavily in the closed-loop economy if they are not clear how far a government wishes recycling to go.

The hole at the centre of policy has also had consequences within Whitehall. There has been no coherent approach running across government. As a result, throughout the 1990s, government was fragmented. Departments pursued their own interests, often in conflict. The Department of Trade and Industry (DTI) promoted incineration as an easy way of meeting renewable energy targets rather than encouraging recycling industries as part of a green industrial strategy. The former Department of the Environment, Transport and Roads (DETR) developed its climate change strategy and its policies on regeneration with only passing reference to waste – a lack of connection even within a single Department. The Treasury resisted hypothecation of the landfill tax to permit public sector support for recycling within the central government budget, and left the problem of initial financing unresolved.

As in the time of a weak mediaeval king, the lack of leadership left power in the hands of contending public and private baronies, none of which had an interest in advancing the new economy. The only coherence was provided by Brussels. Their Directives have become the principal drivers of waste policy in the UK. Lacking confidence in innovation, Whitehall has been preoccupied with how to manage the Directives within the context of the British model of light government and the multiple conflicting interests. Britain has not only remained a follower in waste policy, but has acted as a conservative force in the formation of the Directives themselves, arguing for lower targets, extended time periods, and in some instances discouraging Directives in the first place.

Secondly, the lack of a government identity has meant that it has looked to the established interests to advise on ways to meet the Directives put out by Brussels. The advice that was given has been in terms that reproduce the existing structures. It is not a question of policy being private sector- as against public sector-led, but rather one of how to introduce policies which require major changes in both the public and the private sectors. The issue is old and new, not private and public. In transitions of this kind the problem is that the new has yet to be established. In the endless round of consultations, the interests of the new are barely there to consult.

What this has meant is that the setting of the parameters and the construction of markets – which are the key independent variables in the model of light government – have not been independent at all. Prices in the waste market have not been adjusted to reflect externalities, nor have the flows of public and private resources redirected by government. Neither have planning procedures remained independent. Rather, they have been determined by an implicit policy that, far from encouraging recycling, is in danger of setting limits to its expansion and to the economic and environmental opportunities it opens up.

Thus on the one hand 'light government' has argued that waste policy should be led by a market adjusted to take into account environmental externalities. On the other, the market has been adjusted to reflect a policy formed to meet the Brussels Directives, in consultation with an existing public and private industry whose traditional interests could only be changed by a radical revision of incentives. There is a circularity here. The system of incentives that could help transform an old industry into a new one is set with the advice and on behalf of the old industry to reflect what currently exists. This is the source of the deep conservatism at the heart of British waste policy: it is to be found neither in the civil service, nor in the waste companies, nor the disposal authorities, but rather in a system of government that as far as waste is concerned cannot accommodate the force of the new.

Thirdly, it is finance and statutory regulations rather than indicative targets and information that have influenced the conduct of the industry. As many local authority waste managers pointed out, the 25% recycling target for 2000 was not mandatory and therefore had low priority in cash limited councils. The provision of improved waste data (however necessary) made little impact on waste strategy, nor did the production of recycling plans. Regulations are only as strong as their enforcement and penalties, and both have been weak. It is compulsion and cash – whether in the form of grants, subsidies, taxes or penalties – that have changed behaviour. They need not be alternatives – regulation versus market instruments – but can be linked to each other, as the permit mechanism illustrates.

Lastly, the experiments with privatising the government's public financial functions have each been problematic. The most notorious has been the Landfill Tax Credit scheme. Under the scheme, the Treasury forgoes up to 20% of the revenue due from the tax, if the landfill company chooses to pay the money to an environmental trust for a range of specified purposes. This is a variation on eighteenth century tax farming – in this case the government farming out grant giving to the owners of landfill.

Not surprisingly, the scheme (which is worth £100 million per year) has been subject to gross abuse. Landfill companies and their trade associations have established their own trusts, which they have used to advance their interests (including waste-related road building, research on landfilling and the promotion of incineration). They have used the grants for targeted PR, and have restricted sums going to recycling and to community competitors. Local authorities with access to the funds (for example through clauses in disposal contracts) have used them to finance public services. All this has happened in spite of provisions designed to restrict both the waste companies and the local authorities from abusing the funds. Given the Treasury's concern to control public spending and link it to outcomes, it is astonishing that some £400 million, which would otherwise have been paid to government over the five years of the scheme, has been allowed to be used on miscellaneous projects or the promotion of waste company interests.

The second experiment, the issue and sale of Packaging Recovery Notes, designed to implement the packaging regulations, has also faced difficulties:

- *conflicts over information.* The scheme depends on accurate figures for the quantity of packaging in the waste stream, both in aggregate and for each 'obligated party'. As might be expected, the amount declared by the industry has been less than that estimated by the Environment Agency, and has given rise to lengthy haggling between the two;

- *minimising costs, not advancing a strategy.* The scheme was established not to contribute to the costs of conversion by funding kerbside collection schemes of domestic packaging as in Germany, but to minimise the costs of complying with the EU Directive. This has meant that the targets up to now have been loose, and have been met largely from industrial and commercial waste and more recently from expanding bring banks for domestic waste. As the Chief Executive of VALPAK put it, 'There has been an excess of supply over demand, so therefore the targets, you could argue, have not been tight enough. They should have been set much tighter in retrospect.'[70] The scheme has been successful in its purpose of cost minimisation. UK packagers are contributing less than one-tenth as much as their German counterparts. But Britain's packaging recycling has only increased modestly since the scheme was started (see Table 6).

Table 6 Estimated packaging recycling rates in the UK 1998-2006(%)

	1998	1999	2000	2001	2006*
Aluminium	13	14	15	18**	50
Steel	25	30	32		
Glass	23	27	33		70
Paper	47	47	49		60
Plastic	8	12	12	18**	20
Wood			44		N/A.
All recycling	29	33	36	45	60
EfW	4	5	5		-
All recovery	33	38	42	50**	60

Source: DEFRA Consultation Paper on Packaging, Sept 2001
* amended option targets from EU   ** minimum target

Britain's packaging recycling rate is less than half that of Germany and there is doubt whether it will meet its legal recovery target by the end of 2001.

- *sidelining local authorities*. The scheme was set up explicitly to marginalise local authorities. Money was paid into the scheme by the packaging-related firms in the form of the purchase of packaging recovery notes, a marketable certificate issued by processing firms to say that they had received secondary materials for recycling. This was in effect a quasi-money, and processors were given the profits of the mint. They did not have to give these notes to local authorities that supplied them with materials, only to industry bodies representing the packagers if they supplied recyclable materials. The result is that economic power in this quasi-market has been placed in the hands of processors and the 'obligated' packaging firms,[7] and few of the contributions that have been paid out have gone to local authorities. Much of the profit has remained as a windfall to processors who were already receiving substantial flows of recyclate.

The third scheme, the Private Finance Initiative (PFI), has been even more problematic. As studies undertaken for the DTI pointed out, the construction of large waste facilities, particularly incinerators, was in any case almost all undertaken, owned and financed by the private sector, and underwritten by a local authority-guaranteed gate fee. It was difficult therefore to argue that there could be an extra productivity advantage from private provision using private finance when this was already the norm in the industry. Until September 2000, the seven PFI schemes that had been approved provided large subsidies for incinerator-led packages of provision, whose impact was not to encourage private finance into formally publicly financed projects, but to introduce a bias towards capital-intensive waste plant, contrary to the knowledge-intensive needs of recycling.

All three schemes have similar characteristics. They are innovative experiments in privatising the functions of public finance, they have (with the partial exception of PFI) kept down the size of the public sector budget, and they have each led to a serious squandering of an estimated £1 billion of resources that could have provided the finance necessary to fund the conversion to recycling.

Conclusions

The argument of this chapter is that Britain's failure in recycling is primarily due to the model of light government in place throughout the 1990s. The traditional waste industry cannot be expected to introduce innovations when the incentives are perverse and recycling threatens established functions and interests. It was the responsibility of the government to change the incentives and promote institutions that had an interest in and commitment to the change. Yet it was reluctant to take this on, save when forced to do so by Brussels. What is surprising is that a model of government that is primarily economic in conception failed to address the perverse system of incentives that has been at the root of the problem.

Given this administrative context, and in the absence of a politically significant external environmental movement, no British Government in the 1990s was able to establish strong targets or innovative institutions which would drive the transition to a new waste paradigm. UK waste policy remained oriented to problems of disposal and to the formal fulfilment of EU Directives. As a result Britain finds itself tied to a policy that is now threatening to abort intensive recycling and Zero Waste for a generation.

VIII **The integrated option**

As a result of the failure to expand recycling, an alternative policy emerged, which came to govern both central government policy and that of the great majority of waste disposal authorities in the UK. It now stands blocking the path of intensive recycling, and is the focus of increasingly bitter dispute throughout England, Wales and Northern Ireland.

The policy is similar to those advanced in the face of perceived landfill shortages in the USA and Germany in the late 1980s. Its centrepiece is the construction of a new generation of incinerators. Estimates of the numbers required vary. The Environment Agency's regional waste plans forecast the need for capacity of 18 million tonnes annually, an eightfold increase on current incinerator capacity of 2.3 million tonnes. This is equal to 60 plants of 300,000 tonnes each, or 90 plants of 200,000 tonnes. The model drawn up for the government's Waste Strategy estimated that between 94 and 121 new incinerators of 250,000 tonne capacities would be needed if municipal waste continued to grow at 3%, compared to the 132 estimated in the Landfill Directive RIA model, assuming the same rate of growth and plant capacity.[72]

The forecast numbers vary with the assumed rate of growth, but since incinerators have a lead time of seven to eight years, the municipal waste plans and contracts now being put in place usually assume a 3% rate of growth in their forecasting (in line with municipal waste arising over the past five years) and estimate the size and number of incinerators accordingly.

Given current government planning guidance and the requirements for diversion from landfill, there are few disposal authorities that have not included incineration or some other form of thermal treatment in their long-term waste plans. It suggests that the range of 94 to121 new incinerators given in the Waste Strategy model is the likely outcome in terms of present planning and contract strategies. What this amounts to is a proposal to build incineration capacity of between 27 and 33 million tonnes per annum, sufficient to take all the municipal waste which is now produced.

The current evidence from waste disposal authorities and their unitary counterparts throughout the country is that at a time when a new regulatory framework for minimising waste is being put in place in Europe, and when incineration as an industry is stagnating internationally, Britain is set to embark on the largest new incinerator building programme in the world. Investment costs for a programme of this size are estimated at £8 billion. The waste contracts attached to them have a forecast value of £50 billion. In pursuing this path, Britain now finds itself running against the political, regulatory and industrial tide.

The focus on incineration is the other side of the failure to develop recycling in the UK. Faced with the targets of the Landfill Directive, neither the government, nor the disposal authorities nor the major waste industry see that it is possible to meet these targets with recycling alone. Each presents a similar picture: a graph showing the past five years trend line in municipal waste extending to 2020; a second line describing the landfill diversion targets over the same period and a third one showing the maximum likely level of recycling. Between the assumed level of recycling and the targeted levels of diversion is a gap, one that it is suggested can only be filled by incineration or a similar form of capital-intensive treatment.

This simple model of forecasting is now driving waste strategy at every level in Britain. It has come to be known as the 30:50:40 model, with recycling usually accounting for 30%-35% of total waste arisings (40% in the more ambitious schemes), processing for 40-60%, and landfill for 30%-50%, the totals adding to plus or minus 120% because of the need to process and then landfill part of the residual waste.

The strategies based on this model are referred to as 'the integrated option'. They comprise the three elements of the forecasting model:

- low-road recycling, in the form of mixed waste recycling, bring banks and supplementary multi-material kerbside collections;

- an expansion of some form of mixed waste treatment (principally incineration, supplemented by other types of thermal treatment, and/or anaerobic digestion);

- continued landfill, since all these treatment methods have substantial residues that for the most part are unacceptable as recyclate (incinerators have a bypass of incombustible waste plus ash that amounts to 45% of the waste tonnage for treatment; mixed waste composting produces a low quality output which at the moment is not permitted even as landfill cover).[73]

The standard arrangement is for all three to be combined in a single municipal contract running for 20-25 years. To guard against possible shortfalls in the supply of waste for the incinerator, they are required to include minimum tonnage contracts and a guaranteed gate fee, on the basis of which the contractor can raise finance for the construction of the incinerator. Contracts of this kind effectively protect the financiers and operators of the facilities from the dangers of waste diversion, and from competitors for waste. Where this has not taken place, as in a number of the US states, in Germany and in Switzerland, incinerators have found themselves short of waste and have had to import waste or, in some cases, to close down.

The timing and length of the contracts are determined by the incineration component, as are the companies who bid for them. Only the large old-order waste firms are in a position to bid for and operate a contract of this size. To date this has meant that the recycling and composting components are provided as large-scale facilities established to meet the targetted requirements of the contract.[74]

The attraction of these arrangements for the existing order should be immediately clear. The priority given to disposal, to fixed investment, and to technologies for mixed waste treatment all fit within the existing organisational and technical paradigm. In this sense they appear to be a more reliable option than recycling. Combined in a single package, they are easier for a disposal authority to administer than multiple 'unbundled' contracts, they are more straightforward to finance, and they confirm the disposal authority as the dominant institution in the management of waste.

There are, however, profound environmental problems with this option:

- waste is still viewed as 'end of pipe' and managed from the vantage point of the terminus of linear production. In spite of the new language of resource recovery and waste minimisation, the driving problematic of the industry remains disposal;

- the mass production paradigm which governs the industry cannot cope with the complexity of the processes required to achieve high material and energy productivity;

- thermal treatment, by whatever method, remains problematic because of the fluctuations in feedstock and the control of hazardous emissions to air, water and land that are produced;

- the traditional model of environmental regulation, which is designed to reduce the hazards of waste disposal, is itself limited, reflecting as it does the old paradigm of production that it is seeking to control.

These limitations leave the strategy open to criticism on all three of the main environmental criteria. Pollution problems are not eliminated. The majority of recyclable material is still lost to disposal, as is the grey energy contained within it.

The integrated option is a way of preserving a modified 'business as usual' at substantially higher cost. It represents a major environmental opportunity foregone.

There are also a number of practical problems:

- incinerators are unpopular. The strength of anti-incinerator feeling and its political consequences is one of the main reasons why the building of incinerators has virtually stopped in English-speaking countries and why previous national programmes to use incinerators to fill the gap between expected waste growth and recycling have had to be abandoned. As the waste industry acknowledges, only one new incinerator has been built in the UK in the past ten years;

- the current and future Directives extending producer responsibility and promoting recycling and composting threaten the size of the residual waste stream. By 2010 the achievement of the proposed level of recycling for packaging, increased recycling of newsprint and the separate collection of organics as set out in the draft for the Bio Waste Directive are likely to cut the residual waste stream by 50%, irrespective of other methods of reduction. The risks entailed are borne by the disposal authority;

- the costs associated with other fiscal and regulatory changes also fall to the disposal authority, as the cost of incinerator upgrades have done in the past. Possible changes of this kind include: further upgrading of emissions control; the reclassification of incinerator fly ash as hazardous and bottom ash as special waste; further increases in the landfill tax; the introduction of a tax on incinerators as part of a more general disposal tax; the declassification of pyrolysis and gasification plants as sources of renewable energy; and increased costs to the operator of more rigorous enforcement, including the introduction of continuous monitoring and compulsory public liability insurance for incinerator operators;

- single contracts over 20-25 years bind an authority in to a waste company which may be competent at managing an incinerator, but is not an effective operator of recycling and composting plants. The contracts present a long-term barrier against the adoption of current best practice in recycling and composting technology, where it is not in the interests or the capacity of the contractor to adopt it.

The costs entailed in these risks and rigidities fall outside the gate fee settled in the initial stages of the contract. If they were factored in, for example through mandatory insurance, then the thermal treatment options would be likely to become prohibitively expensive.[75]

From the viewpoint of Zero Waste, the primary drawback of the integrated option is that it places a cap on the expansion of recycling. This is not just a formal cap, based on the percentage of waste guaranteed to the incinerator. Nor is it just a question of a conflict over materials – although an incinerator will seek to preserve recyclable paper and plastic which raise the thermal value of the combustible waste stream.[76] The real issue is that long-term 'integrated' contracts centred on an incinerator preclude the development of the new approach to recycling and clean production that is the subject of this book. Incineration and Zero Waste represent two alternative paradigms that are in continuous tension.

The principal case for the integrated option is that high levels of recycling are impossible. Even were levels of 60% to be achieved this would still leave 40% of the waste as residual, which would need some form of treatment, not least to meet the EU targets. Depending on the assumed rate of waste growth, the required incinerator capacity could be assessed and the size restricted in the contract. This is the core argument. Other parts of the case – about the composition of municipal waste, the assessment of overseas experience, and the likely rates of waste growth – follow from that.

As presented to planning inquiries, citizens' juries, parliamentary debates and Select Committees, the integrated option has raised other, wider issues, such as the relative costs and safety of incineration compared to intensive recycling, and its relative environmental value. Table 7 summarises the arguments presented for the integrated option and those advanced for intensive recycling.

In the end, however, it is not an issue of costs, or environmental and economic benefit. Few people now claim, as many did in the 1990s, that incineration is on a par with recycling in the waste hierarchy. Those arguing for the integrated option can readily agree that recycling and composting are environmentally preferable to incineration, that they generate more jobs, that they cost less in the long run and that they are more popular and create space for citizen involvement.

For the advocates of incineration these points are not relevant, since incineration and recycling are not in competition. As they stress, incineration takes over where recycling stops. The only point at issue is a practical one: namely the maximum level that can be expected for recycling. This defines the point at which the integrated option begins, since it is driven by one overriding question – namely what can be done with the residual.

At the moment there is an impasse on the issue. Those responsible for disposal are incredulous that recycling rates of 40% let alone 60% can be achieved in the UK.[77] Consultants' reports have been commissioned to examine the robustness of claims to high recycling, and to identify supposed reasons why they are not applicable here. The excuses are varied: one high performer has user pay (Switzerland). Another has large suburban gardens (Canberra). A third is small town/rural and not comparable to large urban areas (Quinte). A fourth includes large quantities of commercial waste in its municipal totals and the results cannot be compared. A fifth may be a city but it is Canadian or German and the culture is different from that in Britain.

These inquiries are defensive. They are not intended to learn from best practice in order to adapt it here at home. Their aim is rather to establish a limit to recycling (whether 40% or 70% of the waste stream is in a sense immaterial), so that a planning space is defined in which disposal options can be pursued in isolation as before. The maximum recycling rate forms a frontier between two separate economies, which are not operationally integrated at all.

Behind the studies of recycling rates, waste growth and landfill capacity, lies a quest for certainty – the certainty needed for planning long life, capital-intensive, inflexible facilities. But if one thing is clear from all the discussions of the last five years, it is that so little is certain.

I have already touched on some of the uncertainties with respect to technology and regulation. There is, too, uncertainty over waste growth, over its future composition, over the changing nature of materials, over the extent and impact of producer responsibility, and of the hazards associated with different forms of waste treatment. We do not know where the corporate attention to Zero Waste will lead, or the shift to biodegradable packaging, or to home delivery and take-back, any more than the Germans could have predicted in 1990 that their waste would fall by 36% in six years and that their incinerators would be starved of waste.

Equally, there are uncertainties about recycling and composting. It may be that the systems of Canberra, or San Francisco or the Milan region cannot be transferred to Oldham and Tower Hamlets. On the other hand, Tower Hamlets, with 70% of its residents living in high-rise blocks, may find a method of recycling like that of Hounslow, which will be more effective and cheaper than any low-rise alternative.

The likely shape of the next twenty years cannot be settled now. The question is how to proceed amidst such uncertainty, particularly where the environmental stakes are so high. There are two key words: flexibility and timing. Flexibility has been post-Fordism's answer to uncertainty. If the future is unpredictable, then concentrate on mobility and keeping options open. Investment in large capital-intensive treatment plants runs right against the trends in the modern knowledge economy of keeping fixed assets flexible and investing in information- and knowledge-based service capacity.[78]

At the very moment of the most rapid change in the nature and use of materials, the incinerator programme threatens to freeze the future for a generation. Large thermal plants are a mid-twentieth century response to a twenty-first century circumstance. As such, they risk being stranded by change.

The issue of flexibility is also linked to timing. Incinerators and large-scale capital projects take seven to eight years to bring on-stream. A four-stream recycling system can be in place within a year. The current pressure on local authorities to conclude incinerator-based disposal contracts is such that, given long lead times, early decisions have to be made to meet landfill targets ten to fifteen years ahead. The mammoth of the future comes back to block the present.

Disposal authorities and the national governments of England, Wales, Scotland and Northern Ireland should follow a different timetable. They should focus all energies on establishing four-stream systems, declaring a moratorium on long-term disposal contracts for five years. By the review year of 2006/7 the pre-treatment gap between achieved diversion and the 2010 targets can be better judged and filled with short lead time facilities, and the same goes for the 2015 targets.

Table 7 Key issues in UK Waste Strategy and contrasting approaches

Topic	Argument of incinerator-led strategies	Intensive recycling approach
Waste growth	High and sustained No disaggregation to identify which if any waste is growing	Need to disaggregate to identify which streams/materials are growing, to assess most suitable form of treatment Key role of trade waste diverted into household stream since 1996
Waste composition	Use of early 1990s national data with low biodegradables and aggregate categories 56% recyclable	Hand sorted waste composition studies, showing high organics 30-45 categories differentiated 80%-85% immediately recyclable
Upper limit to recycling	35%-40%	Rates of 50%-60% readily achievable, rising over 10-20 years
Link between recycling and disposal	Recycling and disposal in separate compartments. Strict boundary between the two	Focus diversion on hazardous and biodegradable waste from landfill Rapid diversion programmes to preserve landfill space Flexible disposal options
Landfill	Lowest in hierarchy Emphasise shortage of landfill space	Landfill fine for inert, non-hazardous waste Priority to remove non-inert Critical view of landfill availabilty figures
Incineration & health	Modern incinerators safe and well regulated No evidence of new incinerators causing ill health	Significant emissions to air, and toxicity of ash (also danger to water) Repeated failure of regulation Evidence of health impact of toxic gases/elements coming from incinerators
Incinerators and crowding out	Incinerators sized in accordance with maximum recycling levels	Difficult to prevent crowding out for organisational, professional, financial and technical reasons Incinerators want paper and plastic for high calorific values

Flexibility and incineration	Flexibility issue does not arise because incinerators sized solely for long-term residuals	Incinerators require minimum tonnages and 20-25 year contracts. Monopoly of municipal solid waste (MSW) quantities at time of rapid change Size sets ceiling on recycling Need incinerator moratorium
Other disposal technologies	Gasification and pyrolysis as favoured alternatives (plus anaerobic digestion)	Thermal treatment of mixed waste has faced technical difficulties, and has toxic ash and air/water emission problems
Recycling	Limited potential Play down performance elsewhere or argue exceptional circumstances Favour more capital intensive recycling (centralised sorting) Low value recycling & pressure for reclassification (e.g. ash)	Rapid high recycling possible Learn from best practice at home & overseas Barriers as challenges
Composting	Limited because of low organic volumes and public reluctance to source-separate. Stress dangers from bio-aerosols	Home composting plus separate doorstep collection with neighbourhood closed-vessel compost systems
Disposal Contracts	Long-term and inclusive (aim also to include collection, CA sites and trade in disposal contracts)	Short-term to ensure flexibility Bespoke contracts for different functions
Economics	Incineration same cost as landfill Recycling high cost and persistent	Recycling declining cost industry. Intensive system cuts waste budgets. Issue is financing transition. Incineration and landfill have uncosted risks borne by client authority or public. Should fall to contractor or be mandatorily insured
Economic growth	Not discussed	Green industrial revolution for waste reduction. Recycling creates green-collar jobs and import-substituting reprocessing industry

Climate change and materials saving	Significance played down. No generalisation possible: BPEO for each case. Static LCAs. Incinerators save CO2. Better to burn paper than recycle it	Waste reduction & recycling can have major impact on CO2 reduction and materials savings. Cuts in CO2 from substituting virgin materials greatly outweigh reductions resulting from power generation from thermal treatment. Clear environmental benefits of recycling, composting & minimisation. Dynamic LCAs
Overall strategy	Integrated/'balanced' approach including all main management options	Recycling- and composting-led, with industrial co-operation on ecodesign and waste minimisation. Detoxify landfill
Disposal strategy	Immediate action for new disposal facilities because of long lead time for incinerators	Rapid diversion to safeguard existing landfill capacity. Detoxify residual waste stream. Moratorium on incineration to focus on diversion. Use of MBT.
Planning	Streamlined planning procedures to avoid hold-ups in permission for new thermal treatment. Environment Agency continues to assess polluting aspects of proposals	Need for community concensus for waste initiatives. Planning should include assessment of impact of pollution (currently the primary responsibility of the Environment Agency). Financial support to community in assessing plans
Implementation	Strengthening powers of disposal and central authorities, particularly through RTABs	Zero Waste Trusts with funding flows to multiple delivery agents. Strong role for community sector

Government policy and inflexible integration

The implicit government policy that emerged during the 1990s was to support 'the integrated option'. Whatever the wording of the White Papers giving primacy to waste minimisation, the central thrust of policy, finance and planning was to solve the disposal problem through incinerator-led packages.

Incineration faced three practical issues if it was to take its place at the centre of such packages: these related to its environmental credentials; its expense relative to landfill; and the difficulties of getting planning permission because of its unpopularity. The UK Government devoted more time to addressing these questions during this period than it did to promoting recycling.

(i) policy

The arguments advanced in favour of incineration have followed those summarised in the first column of Table 7:

- modern incinerators are safe;

- they make a significant contribution to the reduction of CO_2 through energy recovery, and even more so when they supply district heating. In relation to energy and the Kyoto targets it is EfW rather than recycling that has been emphasised. The saving of energy from replacing primary with secondary materials from recycling was omitted from the principal study undertaken for the DETR on the significance of waste policy for climate change;[79]

- incinerators may be environmentally and economically preferable in certain circumstances. In the words of the 1995 White Paper, EfW 'will increasingly represent the best practicable environmental option (BPEO) for many wastes. This will especially be the case where final disposal becomes more limited and in situations where the environmental and economic costs (including collection and transport) of recycling are high and where the practical optimum for materials recovery has been reached.'[80]

For this argument to hold, much depended on life cycle analysis as applied to particular materials, waste management methods and places. The second half of the 1990s thus saw an increasing use of these tools to determine the BPEO, largely using static LCAs, and culminating in the Environment Agency's WISARD, a model that disposal authorities were required to use to determine the optimum mix of methods.

On the basis of these three arguments, local authorities were encouraged to include EfW in their disposal plans and to consider the need for long-term disposal contracts as a condition for financing the large-scale investment required.

All three arguments are now in question. The revelations about the operating conditions at the Byker and Edmonton incinerators, of the exceedances and the practices of ash disposal, have raised major questions about the safety of 'actually existing incinerators'. These concerns have been compounded by the fires at the Dundee incinerator and the Wolverhampton plant, and by the problems of persistent exceedances at the Coventry and Sheffield plants.[81] The precautionary principle now hangs like a cloud over the safety claims about modern incinerators as they actually operate.

Secondly, the US EPA 1998 report and the idea of environmental opportunity cost would counsel prudence in arguing for EfW's contribution to CO_2 reduction, relative to recycling and composting.

Similarly the critique of static LCAs and the controversy surrounding WISARD makes the concept of BPEO a less reliable support for EfW than was once thought.

(ii) finance

The principal practical problem for incineration has been its high cost relative to landfill, an underlying differential that has increased as emissions limits have tightened. The government – through both the former DETR and the DTI – has concentrated on reducing this gap. The increase in the landfill tax assisted in this. But the two ministries have, between them, provided a range of subsidies or decisions on classification that have lowered the costs of incineration.

The subsidy and classification measures have included:

- awards under successive tranches of the NFFO, which for the two London incinerators alone were worth £14 million p.a.;

- exemption of incineration from the proposed Climate Change levy;

- the inclusion of pyrolysis and gasification in the Renewables Obligation;

- the provision of government funds under the Private Finance Initiative;

- the classification of incinerator bottom ash as inert, thus reducing the landfill tax to £2 a tonne;

- the classification of incinerator ash for construction purposes as recycling (ceased 2001) and the promotion of its use as a means of reducing the costs of disposal;

- the classification of energy from waste as recovery rather than disposal. (The EU Commission argued that it was disposal, on the grounds that the low thermal value of municipal solid waste did not qualify it to be considered as a fuel.) This allowed EfW plants to issue and sell packaging recovery notes for the packaging element of their combusted waste (a proportion estimated at 19%);

- the exemption from business rates;

- the provision of normal capital allowances on all forms of fixed investment.

The sums involved, estimated at £1 billion over seven years, dwarfed those provided for recycling.[82] In cases where there was an opportunity to fund intensive household recycling, through the Landfill Tax compliance scheme or the packaging regulations, local authorities and recycling collection were marginalised.

(iii) **planning**

The process of obtaining the necessary planning permission and consents has been a significant hurdle for the constructors of incinerators. The government used two main approaches to ease the process:

- it encouraged local authorities to include EfW in their waste local plans, (current planning guidance, PPG 10, specifies that local authorities should make provision for all forms of waste treatment, a clause frequently quoted in planning inquiries in support of incinerator applications);[83]

- there has been persistent pressure for the environmental and health impacts of an incinerator application to be dealt with solely by the Environment Agency under the IPPC regulations, a move which leaves them less open to public scrutiny than in the customary planning process.

Throughout the 1990s there was strong official support for a revival of incineration. In 1993, the Royal Commission on Environmental Pollution advocated the increased use of incineration with energy recovery for the disposal of controlled waste, and the 1995 White Paper endorsed these conclusions.[84] The 1999 Consultation Paper, 'A Way With Waste', although relegating EfW below recycling for the first time in the waste hierarchy as the result of political pressure, nevertheless stated that EfW, 'will need to play a full and integrated part in the local and regional solutions'.[85] It underlined the importance of the 'integrated approach' and the need to include a mixture of waste management options and 'avoid over-reliance on a single waste management option'.[86]

With the focus on re-establishing incineration, the DETR and the DTI had little time and less money to advance recycling. In using public funds and directives to level the economic playing field between landfill and incineration, it tilted it further away from early stage recycling, relative to incineration. The resulting poor performance of recycling confirmed the view of the limitations of recycling and gave even greater significance to alternative disposal options. In this sense the policy, financial and planning frameworks all combined towards a self-fulfilling recycling pessimism, leading to the current dominant option being that of 'inflexible integration'.

Changes in political climate

Early in 2000, the politics of waste began to change. Until then, local campaigns against incinerators and in favour of recycling had remained local. They received wide coverage in their local press, but scarcely any nationally. In March 2000, the Guardian carried the first coverage of the ash scandal at the Byker incinerator in Newcastle. In May the results of the independent testing of the ash and allotment soils on which the ash had been spread were announced, and filled the national press.

Since then not only the broadsheets, but BBC radio and television have covered waste stories, from alleged corruption in the Landfill Tax Credit scheme and the continuing revelations about Byker and Edmonton ash, to the growing number of anti-incinerator campaigns in Surrey, Sussex, Kent, Essex, Cornwall, Kidderminster, Wrexham, Liverpool, Lancashire, Sheffield, Humberside, Newcastle and Neath Port-Talbot.

At Byker and Neath, protestors chained themselves to the incinerator gates. At Edmonton and Sheffield, Greenpeace occupied the chimneys. A national network was formed in May 2001, bringing together all these groups in Britain and Ireland. In July 2001 Greenpeace was acquitted of charges of criminal damage by a north London jury, on the grounds that its crime was justified since it was preventing greater harm to those living near the plant.

The strength of local feeling was reflected politically. In May 2000, the Conservative Party published a waste policy that proposed a five-year moratorium on incineration, kerbside recycling for every home in Britain, and a dense network of compost sites throughout the country. The Liberal Democrats published a similar manifesto at the same time.

From mid-2000 there was a marked change in government policy. It departed from the 'light government' approach in three principal ways:

1. compulsory recycling targets for local authorities were included in the Waste Strategy 2000 in May 2000;

2. the first specialised recycling institution was announced in the Strategy, the Waste Resources Action Programme (WRAP), to promote markets for recyclate;

3. the Spending Review in July 2000 announced direct government support for recycling, reportedly in excess of £500 million over three years, supplemented by £50 million for community recycling schemes.

In the areas of targets and finance, there were administrative moves to weaken the support of these measures for recycling. The targets were set much lower than was hoped (25% in 2005, 30% in 2010 and 33% in 2015) in line with the maximum levels officials believed could be achieved, and consistent with '30:50:40' packages being advanced under the integrated option.

More strikingly, it was found that DETR officials had classified incineration ash used in road building and construction as recycling, with the result that those authorities with large incinerators rose overnight to the top of the recycling league.

Similarly, when the Spending Review allocations were broken down, it transpired that £220 million was to be allocated to PFI waste projects, all of which to that date had been incinerator-led packages, £140 million was reserved for recycling, and the remainder was part of a package of £1.127 million allocated to local authorities to spend on environmental and cultural services at their discretion. Given the relatively weak position of recycling within the context of local authority budgetary politics, this left collection authority waste officers with few potential earmarked funds on which to base a radical re-orientation of their collection systems, so that an important opportunity for promoting recycling was lost.[87]

In spite of these difficulties, the shift in government outlook was marked. WRAP was established rapidly and appointed as its leading adviser the principal US expert on secondary material market creation. In October 2000, the Government 'de-listed' incineration as eligible under the Renewables Obligation (although as a compromise pyrolysis and gasification were still included).

The proposed shift in the EU packaging targets from recovery to recycling signals the end of the PRN subsidy for incinerators. The Parliamentary Select Committee that considered Waste Policy, reporting in March 2001, urged the Government to adopt the more ambitious recycling targets of 50% by 2010 and 60% by 2015, and re-iterated the call of an earlier Select Committee to impose a tax on incineration as part of a more general disposal tax. The Welsh Assembly in May 2001, as part of its response to the Kyoto targets, agreed a planning 'presumption against' incineration to secure the space for the development of 'recycling and sustainability'[88].

Concerned over the widening conflict over waste strategy throughout the country, and the lack of progress being made in meeting the EU Landfill Directive's diversion targets, the Government called a Waste Summit in November 2001, and announced a review of policy to be undertaken by the Performance and Innovation Unit in the Cabinet Office.

None of this is yet sufficient to slow the momentum behind the incinerator-led plans and contracts being advanced by the disposal authorities. Yet it signals a change in the political climate, which provides the context for immediate measures that would switch Britain's waste economy from its current preoccupation with incineration to intensive recycling and the advance of each of the aspects of Zero Waste.

IX A Zero Waste Policy for Britain

The second term Labour Government has announced that it will focus on delivery. Waste is a sector in which it can tangibly deliver. To do so it will have to radically extend the initiatives of the past two years, and to provide leadership both for its civil servants and those involved in the day-to-day management of waste.

The municipal sector

Municipal waste represents only just over a quarter of industrial, commercial and municipal waste combined (and only 7% of total waste if agricultural, mining and construction waste is taken into account). But it is the starting point for an alternative policy for three reasons:

- government has a more direct influence over the way waste is managed in the municipal sector;

- municipal recycling and composting provides a core infrastructure which should be made available for industrial and commercial waste;

- household waste is the interface between citizens and the waste problem. It affects everyone. If the problems of waste do not start under the kitchen sink, they can be seen there, as can part of the solution. Recycling provides a way for everyone to contribute to alternative environmental policies. It is a form of productive democracy, whose impact extends beyond the home, to work, to public spaces and to the ballot box.

For these reasons, the first step towards Zero Waste is to change the way in which municipal waste is managed. In the UK this requires two major sets of changes:

- a shift in strategy from intensive incineration to intensive recycling, from 'inflexible fragmentation' to 'flexible integration';

- the introduction of measures to put this strategy into practice.

Intensive recycling

Municipal waste needs to be re-oriented around four primary policies:

1. The diversion and composting of organic waste

The first aim of the initial stage of the UK's conversion programme should be to:

- **introduce separate organic collections throughout the UK by 2006 together with a network of local closed vessel composting units**

Hand sorted studies of the composition of UK municipal waste suggest that organics account for between 30% and 45% of dustbin waste, and some 40% of civic amenity waste. Diverting a high proportion of this waste should be a first target. In addition to the environmental benefits, there is another technical reason for the importance of this approach. By reducing the fermentable element in residual waste, it makes a switch to fortnightly collections possible, and transforms the economics of diversion.

The key change that is needed is that proposed for implementation throughout the EU in the Commission's draft Bio Waste Directive: separate kerbside organic collections. Introducing this immediately in this country would shift the UK from the bottom quartile of European recyclers to the upper half, alongside regions and countries already collecting organics (the Netherlands, Flanders, Germany, Austria and a growing number of regions in Italy). It would make Britain a leader, not a follower, of European policy. It would also ensure that all authorities met their recycling targets by 2005/6.

The most effective model for organic collection to date is that developed in Italy (see inset 1). It is centred on a low-cost food waste collection system, home composting and a supplementary periodic garden waste collection service at weekends. More than 1,000 municipalities have adopted this system in all parts of Italy, in many cases with a reduction in waste costs.

2. The diversion of dry recyclables

- multi-material kerbside collections of dry recyclables should be extended to all households in the UK and current average capture rates should be doubled

The highest rates of capture of dry recyclables are achieved by multi-material kerbside collection (MMKC). Even a dense system of bring banks will nowhere match the capture rate of properly resourced kerbside schemes.

Currently only 19% of available dry recyclables in the dustbins of England and Wales are being source-separated. This is mainly due to the low level of MMKC. While 44% of all households have some form of kerbside collection of dry recyclables, many of them are sporadic, single material, not user friendly, and geared more to minimising cost than maximising recovery. Only 3% are served by multi-material collections.

The national average weight of dry recyclables collected at the kerbside for all households is 32 kg p.a. out of an estimated 336 kg p.a. in the dustbin. The average for all existing kerbside schemes is 73 kg per household serviced p.a, and 94 kg for multi-material collections. Well run kerbside schemes should capture 120-140kg per household p.a. in their early stages and build up to 200-230kg per household p.a. as the scheme matures.[89]

Policy should be focussed on doubling the number of households covered by kerbside collections and doubling the amount captured from each household served through extending the coverage and effectiveness of multi-material collection.

Inset 2

Italian food waste collection systems

Although the first initiative to collect food waste separately in Italy took place in 1993, the main cause of its expansion has been the 1997 Waste Management Law, which set recycling targets of 35% for local authorities to achieve by 2003. This target made it necessary to separate organic waste. In Northern Europe kerbside organic collections accept garden waste and food waste in the same container (usually a dedicated organic wheeled bin). The Italian innovation has been to treat them separately.

The argument for this is that food waste is the priority. It is the main contaminator of what the Italians call 'restwaste' in the regular dustbin. Once food is removed, restwaste does not have to be collected so often, and its fermentability in landfills – which is the major problem for emissions – is radically reduced.

Focusing on food waste also allows for much cheaper and more effective collection systems. Because food waste has a high density and water content, it does not need compaction. As a result the Italians have developed small micro vehicles, with a 3-5 cu metre capacity, and costing between 10%-15% of an ordinary refuse lorry.

The food waste vehicle shown is from the commune of Cupello in the Abruzzi region on the Adriatic, and is one of the larger models. It can be operated by a single person, collecting 3-4 tonnes a day from some 2000 households. Residents place their waste in small plastic bags in a six-litre bin near the sink. This is then transferred to a 30-litre collection bucket that can be easily lifted by hand. The bags are transparent to allow the collector to check their content, and are biodegradable so that they rot down with the food.

The vehicle has a bin lift on the back so that food waste, placed in the water tight bags, can be collected on the same rounds from wheeled bins at apartment buildings as well as restaurants and food shops. The vehicle also has a tipping mechanism, so that once it is full, it can offload into an ordinary refuse lorry for long distance carrying to the central compost plant. A further cost saving could be made by developing local closed vessel compost systems which could be fed by the micro vehicles directly.

The average yield of the food waste schemes is 150-200 kg per household per year, or from 60%-80% of food waste in the average dustbin. Little if any of this is garden waste (not least because of the small size of the plastic bags). Garden waste is largely composted at home or taken to civic amenity sites. The Italians argue that providing mixed organic or garden waste collections makes it easy for householders not to compost their garden waste and invariably increases the quantity of waste that a local authority has to handle. The iron law of garden waste is that special collections increase the recycling rate but also total waste arisings. In some instances, Italian councils provide a fortnightly or monthly garden waste service, usually with a charge, using a regular off duty compactor at weekends.

Many of the municipalities who have adopted this model have achieved 50% recycling levels. The food waste collections have commonly saved money, since a food waste team may cost as little as a third of that of an ordinary refuse round, yet service the same number of households. The halving of rest waste collection frequencies therefore releases resources from which the food waste collections can be funded.

The system has also provided a high quality feedstock for compost, (with contamination rates of only 2%, significantly lower than the wheeled bin systems in Northern Europe), the need for which is reflected in the fact that three Italian regions now provide subsidies of up to £120 a tonne for the application of compost on agricultural land.

3. The recycling of bulky waste

- the disposal-oriented system of civic amenity sites should be converted to a dispersed network of reuse and recycling centres, integrated with regular doorstep collections of bulky items

Bulky waste, including consumer durables, rubble, wood, scrap metal, cardboard and garden waste, is largely disposed of through civic amenity sites, supplemented by special collections, pick-ups as part of weekly dustbin collections, and fly tipping. Civic amenity waste alone accounts for 23% of household waste or some 275 kg per household p.a.

Since they were first established over thirty years ago, civic amenity sites have been designed primarily as drop-off sites for disposal. Under the Environmental Protection Act of 1990, it is the responsibility of disposal authorities to provide such drop-off points. Many households have no ready access to these sites – particularly in cities where property prices are high, and in rural areas – or where a household has no car.

Many CA sites now have containers in which householders can deposit source-separated materials for recycling. The diversion rate on CA sites in England and Wales has risen to nearly 20%, with a growing number of authorities reaching 50-60%, and some exceeding 70%.

The aim in the UK should be to raise the average recycling rate of bulky waste to 60% by 2005/6. This will entail:

- increasing the number of sites to a density of one per 30,000 households in urban areas and one per market town in rural areas;

- re-designing the sites as reuse and recycling centres, with layouts that permit vehicle flow, an enclosed area for storage and security and increased staffing for advice and control;

- increased special collection services with free pick-ups for households who separate their waste for recycling;

- a shift of responsibility for civic amenity sites from disposal to collection authorities to allow for their integration with kerbside collections of bulky waste, organics and dry recyclables;

- the co-ordination of bulky waste recycling services with manufacturers and distributors covered by producer responsibility legislation.

4. Management of residual waste through Mechanical and Biological Treatment (MBT)

A central goal of a transition policy for Zero Waste is to 'clean' the residual stream of waste going to landfill. High diversion of organics, supplemented by the recycling of paper, textiles and wood will contribute to this, as will the introduction of special collections of hazardous household waste as part of the recycling and redesigned civic amenity services. But the residual will need further treatment. In the initial years at least, residual waste is likely to contain 15-20% organics even with food waste and garden waste collections.[90] This needs to be neutralised before disposal.

Article 6a of the Landfill Directive requires that 'only (non inert) waste that has been subject to treatment is landfilled'. It states that this be understood in terms of the objectives of the Directive which are to reduce the quantity of waste, or the hazards to human health or the environment. Those countries that have put reduction of environmental pollution at the centre of their waste strategies have interpreted article 6a to mean that the fermentability of all residual waste is reduced to a minimum. Germany has banned the landfilling of all untreated organic waste by 2005. Austria, Italy and Sweden have introduced similar provisions. The UK should do likewise.[91] The government should:

Inset 3

Mechanical and Biological Treatment in Milan

The MBT plant in Milan began production in 1997. It was established in response to a landfill crisis in the mid 1990s, as a means of both reducing the quantity of waste sent to landfill and stabilising its organic element. The plant is the largest in Europe with a capacity of 600,000tpa, and handles all the residual waste from Milan (population 1.6 million).

In MBT plants, the mechanical treatment is normally in two stages. The first is a processing stage where the mixed waste is passed through a drum or pulveriser – often with heat added – in order to loosen the waste and evaporate some of its moisture. The second is a separation stage where materials are recovered through the use of screens, air blowers, magnets and similar processes. The separated organic fraction of the waste is then composted.

In Milan, the mixed waste first moves through a 20mm screen to take out the 'fines'- much of it organic, and through an 80mm screen to remove larger items, mainly paper, cardboard and plastic (the so called 'oversieve'). The remaining 'undersieve' is then treated in a large, hot bio-reactor for 15-20 days (the dry stabilisation method), screened at 40mm, and moved to a second bio-reactor for a further 40 days, prior to a final screening at 10-12 mm to capture the remaining contaminants such as plastic and glass.

As a result of the process, there is an overall loss in weight of 15% (which with landfill at £100 a tonne is a substantial saving) and a reduction of fermentability by 90%. MBT plants can be distinguished according to what they do with the separated materials. Some are oriented towards bio-waste neutralisation, using the grey compost for land reclamation or forestry growth, while others gear the process to producing high calorific feedstock for incinerators. Milan (like the Siggerwiesen MBT plant in Austria) is an example of the former. In both these cases all materials are sent to landfill.

The Milan plant was built rapidly. It started operations in 1997 and the contract runs only until 2003, with the initial investment of £20 million equipment being depreciated over 5 years. At the end of this time the plant can either continue as a mixed waste treatment plant or be converted for the processing of source separated organic waste and further sorting of dry recyclables.

Milan's MBT plant is not an alternative to source separated recycling and composting. The recovered materials have considerable cross contamination. Even the final, sieved, composted fraction has significant quantities of fragmented glass and plastic in it making it unsuitable for agricultural or horticultural use. The function of the plant has been rather to 'neutralise' the residual waste that remains after recycling and composting.

- introduce a ban on untreated municipal waste going to landfill by 2006

All forms of mixed waste treatment have their drawbacks (and hazards) which is why Zero Waste seeks to eliminate all waste for disposal. Treatment plants should therefore be seen as transitional, to be reduced as diversion increases. The principal requirement of treatment technologies is that they should not crowd out recycling and composting, but be geared to respond to the changes in residual waste volumes over the transition period. They should:

- have short capital turnover times (being quick to bring onstream and amortisable rapidly);

- have multipurpose equipment (to allow sections of the plant to process source-separated material as diversion increases and residual volumes fall);

- contribute to environmental goals, notably the reduction of greenhouse gases and of air and water pollution;

- keep treatment costs low over the transition period.

In other words, they should aim to be clean, cheap and flexible.

The method that comes closest to these requirements is mechanical-biological treatment (MBT).[92] MBT plants are now widespread in Germany, Austria and Italy (see inset 2). Through a process of tumbling and screening, organics in the residual waste are separated off and processed in a closed composting plant or anaerobic digester in order to reduce their fermentability by at least 90% of the original level. In the process of screening, some other materials are recovered (such as metal, glass, paper and plastic) and the overall quantity of waste for disposal can be reduced by some 30-40%.

The advantage of MBT plants is that they are a simpler and therefore cheaper option than incinerators and other complex treatment technologies. They are modular, with different equipment being added depending on the type and quality of materials that are to be separated. Much of this equipment and the enclosed compost facilities/digesters can be converted to the treatment of source-separated materials as levels of diversion increase.

Like all mixed waste treatment facilities they need to operate to high health and safety standards, with bio-filters to reduce odours, bioaerosols, and VOCs. If they can be operated to these standards (and much depends on an effective inspectorate) then their advantages make MBT the preferred option to meet the treatment goals by 2006.[93]

The Draft Directive on Composting and Biological Treatment makes clear that those materials that have undergone MBT and achieved the limit values on fermentability, will no longer be considered as 'biodegradable' and hence will be regarded as contributing to the diversion targets of Article 5. A disposal authority and its constituent collection authorities which treats its residuals through an MBT plant will meet the requirements of Articles 5 in addition to those of Article 6 more rapidly, more cheaply and with a more positive environmental impact than any thermal treatment alternative.

Flexible integration

The above strategy stands in contrast to the 'integrated option' that has governed UK policy to date. The contrast is not between a single form of waste management (recycling) and an 'integrated' package. Rather it is between flexible integration and inflexible fragmentation. With incinerator-led packages, the main integration is formal – through a single contract. Strategically and operationally, diversion and disposal remain separated, planned independently of each other, and, as diversion increases, in tension.

With flexible integration on the other hand, recycling priorities are set to reduce the hazards of disposal (hence the emphasis on composting and the separation of hazardous waste), while disposal is planned with technologies which can respond promptly (and economically) to changes in residual tonnages, and with equipment that can be converted for use with source-separated materials as recycling and organic capture rates increase. Where flexible integration has been put into practice, as in Halifax, Nova Scotia (see inset 4), community opposition to new landfills has turned to support because of the twofold character of the strategy: a commitment by the city government to high diversion and a neutralisation of waste going to landfill using MBT.

The conditions for delivery

To deliver the above strategy of flexible integration, four things are needed:

- clear direction

- transformed incentives

- transitional finance

- specialised institutions

The first two are about expectations and interests. The second two are about finance and knowledge. Immediate, decisive action is needed in all four areas if the redirection of Britain's waste economy is to be achieved by 2006.

1. Clarification of goals and strategy

The process of environmental transition gives a privileged place to government direction. It indicates to those making the long-term industrial decisions the character of the regulatory and fiscal regime within which they will be operating. It sets the parameters of the future.

Waste Strategy 2000 does not perform this function. Like the White Papers that preceded it, it contains the language of waste minimisation, but its substance promotes 'the integrated option'. This is partly due to its absences – to what it does not say about finance and incentives – but it is also because of what it does say.

The key sentences – quoted in council meetings and public inquiries throughout the country – are those insisting on the 'important role' of incineration. The words aim to present incineration as subsidiary, but in practice it is always dominant. It determines the length and size of contracts, it restricts the field of contractors, it encourages old era technology, and it signals unequivocally that for the next twenty years there will be an irremovable cap on the expansion of recycling. Whether in London or Stockton, in Lerwick or Birmingham, experience shows that the hare of intensive recycling cannot run with the hounds of incineration. Through the gap opened up by these sentences are pouring proposals that place incineration in the lead.

The core message of Waste Strategy 2000 is the 'integrated option'. This is the perspective shaping the long-term strategies of waste companies and disposal authorities. They are having to take on board the household recycling targets, but these are set at levels which leave 70% of municipal waste available for disposal, a volume which is then compounded by assumptions of two decades of an annual 3% growth.

If the Government wants waste companies and local authorities to redirect their strategies then it must give an unambiguous statement to that effect, especially as what is being signalled is a change of paradigm. It should be made clear that incineration and complex technologies of mixed waste treatment are not the path to be taken and that the problems which the profession should be confronting are those of high quality composting and up-cycling, not how to control emissions and prevent explosions at thermal treatment plants. The Government needs to indicate that it is looking for a new technological trajectory.

Inset 4

Halifax, Nova Scotia

In the late 1980s, the Halifax region in Nova Scotia (population 350,000) faced intense civic opposition to an expansion of its landfill site in Sackville. The joint councils proposed a 500 tonne per day incinerator as an alternative, but this, too, was strongly opposed. The local action groups raised money and hired their own consultants from Seattle who laid out a cheaper, alternative plan for a recycling led strategy. Subsequently, the councils turned down the incinerator proposal because of its costs and its threat to the development of intensive recycling and agreed in principle with the Seattle plan.

They also decided to involve the action groups in designing the scheme. Decisions were made by consensus. The key conclusion from the process was that no organic waste, or toxic waste or recyclables should go to landfill. Anything going to landfill had to first be treated to remove all toxics, organics and recyclables, and to stabilise the remainder through composting.

The system that emerged followed these recommendations. It was a three stream system with all households being served by kerbside collection of dry recyclables, 72% of them having kerbside collection of organics (using special aerated wheeled bins), access to a strong home composting programme plus collection of residuals.

95 Enviro depots were set up to receive beverage containers (all of which other than milk containers have a deposit on them), and there were tyre pick ups from auto stores (the tyres being recycled in a new plant that freezes and produces a high quality crumb rubber). There are drop off sites for hazardous waste, places for the recycling of 2nd hand building materials, a MRF handling 18,000 tonnes a year and two centralised composting sites.

For residual waste there is a screening plant, which pulls out bulky items, recyclables, and toxics, and then stabilises the residual using a trough system with 14 bays. The landfill has been renamed a 'residual disposal facility' and is notable for its lack of odour and birds.

A key development role has been played by the Resource Recovery Fund which acts as promoter of recycling and processing, organises logistics, finances new projects and passes back savings to municipalities.

The result is that Halifax from a diversion level of 3% in 1997, reached 60% within three years. Its drink container system recovered 80% of the deposit containers and 96-98% returns of reusable beer bottles. The main improvements sought locally have been to have smaller, local compost facilities, particularly in the rural areas where the composting could be done by farmers. With a programme to increase capture rates and extend the facilities for the recycling of bulky goods, the civic groups estimate that recycling rates should increase to 88% within ten years.

In shifting the vision, it must also explain the reason for doing so – in terms not of EU Directives but of environmental imperatives, that are likely to intensify as time proceeds. These provide the material basis for the change in strategy, a basis that all governments will have to address whatever their political aesthetic. This, too, requires a change of tone from Waste Strategy 2000.

What is called for is a new White Paper that does three things:

(a) **clarifies the scope and purpose of intensive recycling and the goals of Zero Waste**

It should ground the strategy more firmly in the goals of cleaner production, the global reduction of CO_2, increased resource productivity and soil restitution. These become the criteria of conduct, and should determine the action of each Department of government. Instead of a government policy approach that has argued down targets and weakened Directives, while aiming to meet limited targets at least cost, each Department – and the Environment Agency – should become a promoter of intensive recycling within its sphere of responsibility.

(b) **converts the current local authority recovery targets of 45% by 2010 and 67% by 2015 into mandatory municipal waste recycling targets**

The dropping of recovery goals and their replacement by demanding recycling targets is the present lead proposal for the revision of the 2006 Packaging Targets within the EU. Adopting the conversion proposals for household waste in the UK would put Britain's targets broadly in line with the 50/60% proposals of the Select Committee and would give all those involved in municipal waste a clear signal as to the strategic path to follow.

(c) sets out the fourfold strategy for diversion and treatment for 2006/7

The broad goals and the strategic targets need to be reinforced by an outline of the principal steps to follow. These are the programmes for organics, dry recyclables and bulky waste set out above, and approaches for treating the residual. As far as treatment is concerned there are two priorities:

- the early construction of a new generation of mechanical and biological treatment plants;

- a moratorium on all new forms of thermal treatment until a Strategic Review in 2006/7.

Many of the states and regions that have promoted intensive recycling have done so in conjunction with a ban on incineration, in order to leave space for recycling to take root and to leave no ambiguity about the required change in direction. A similar clear statement is needed in the UK.

The construction of incinerators (and even the potential for construction) creates an interest for the companies and the disposal authorities involved which has consistently come into conflict with strategies for intensive recycling. In the UK this has been evident in the policy debates on waste, in the conflicts between collection and disposal authorities and in the recycling performance of those areas covered by incinerators.

A Zero Waste Strategy needs to focus on the many challenges posed by diversion. It requires a consensus of all those involved – from the householder to waste companies. Recycling and composting have met with widespread support. Incineration has been divisive. Since the function of treatment can be met more flexibly and cheaply through MBT, without the need for long-term contracts, the incineration option is a diversion from the main issues in Zero Waste and should be set to one side.

2. Restructuring incentives

There will be no change on the ground, whatever the wording of a new Strategy, without a radical restructuring of incentives. The long-term shift to producer responsibility for waste is part of this, and the changes already taking place to minimise waste through process and product innovation in the packaging industry exemplify the point.

A complementary shift to consumer responsibility by introducing user pay would also provide an incentive to residual waste minimisation (albeit on a smaller scale). Certainly, overseas experience has often been that introducing user pay helps boost recycling rates. In the UK, this should be a second stage rather than first stage change for two reasons:

- introducing user pay before established, convenient kerbside collections are set up encourages fly-tipping;

- there is already scope for introducing charges and discounts within the terms of current legislation (see Chapter IV, Section 7 above). The inability to charge directly for the collection of residual waste will also encourage innovation by waste collectors in the incentives they offer to householders.

Instead the focus for immediate action should be on changing the incentives to the principal decision takers on waste disposal – the disposal authorities and the waste companies. The first thing that has to be changed is the perverse hierarchy of profitability. If landfill offers the greatest returns (over 15% p.a.) and recycling the least, then it is to be expected that recycling remains the Cinderella sector of the waste industry.

To reverse this there are two issues that need to be kept distinct:

(i) levelling the playing field between recycling and disposal

There are wide divergences in relative costs per tonne between landfill, incineration and the initial stages of recycling. This is the short run position. In the long run, recycling costs fall, and the costs of residual waste management rise (due to tighter environmental controls and increased unit costs as disposal waste volumes fall).

Three steps are necessary to correct the present imbalance between initial recycling and disposal:

- the introduction of a disposal tax with levels reflecting the relative external environmental costs and benefits of each waste option. Studies by the US EPA and Coopers Lybrand for the EU provide a measure of the relative weights to be attached. As a first step, the UK could follow the Danish model, by introducing a further escalator in landfill tax when the current escalator expires, to bring the level up to an average of £30 a tonne. On the USEPA and Coopers Lybrand evidence, the tax on incinerators should be set at or near the figure for landfill;

- ending subsidies and ambiguous classifications designed to lower the costs of incineration This includes ending the exemption of incinerators from the Climate Change levy, ending PFI awards for large scale incinerator-led contracts, and ending the eligibility of incinerators to issue Packaging Recovery Notes;

- internalising risk in disposal contracts by shifting risks to contractors and requiring mandatory insurance for landfills, thermal treatment plants and large composting and recycling facilities as a means of quantifying environmental risk.

(ii) recycling incentives for waste disposal authorities

Currently, waste disposal authorities (other than unitary authorities) have no interest in the expansion of recycling by collection authorities or community groups because they are required to pay the incremental disposal savings to the collector in the form of a recycling credit. An urgent task of policy is to restore an incentive to disposal authorities.

There are the following possibilities:

- a rebate of landfill tax to disposal authorities on tonnages equal to those on which they have paid recycling credits;

- a graduated landfill tax with low rates for base volumes, and rising rates to marginal levels as high as £45 a tonne. This is a variant of the Wallonia model where the regional government offers zero tax landfilling for a proportion of residual waste, and then a high marginal rate. The landfill tax could be extended to a disposal tax by giving rebates for pre-treated waste, scaled to reflect the environmental benefits of the treatment option;

- the replacement of Disposal Authority precepts based on council tax charges by a charge per tonne. This measure would be aimed at disposal authorities owned by constituent boroughs (such as those in London, Merseyside and Greater Manchester) and would apply 'the polluter pays' principle to the funding of disposal authorities. A change of this kind would involve one or more of the constituent authorities suffering a loss, which the government should offer to fund on a four-year tapering basis while the losers increase their rate of waste diversion;

- the combining of collection and disposal functions in a unitary Waste Minimisation Authority charged with advancing the government's strategy and achieving the targets within the area concerned.

3. Finance

Lack of finance is the main disincentive to collection authorities expanding composting and recycling schemes. At any committee meeting, waste hearing or public discussion on recycling, both councillors and officers will cite problems of funding and markets (which is another way of talking about finance) as the two reasons why they cannot at the moment proceed further. In local government terms, this is a budget rather than a price disincentive.

The main counterweight has been provided by local pressure on politicians. As a general rule, an incinerator proposal in any borough or district will increase local resources devoted to recycling. This may be enough to encourage some pioneers: it is not adequate to fund a countrywide transition. If collection authorities are to promote intensive recycling, then they, too, need access to transition finance, on terms that outweigh the disincentives to change.

There are two issues:

- the demand for funds (the requirements of transition finance)

- the source of funds

(a) **the demand for funds**

In the long run, landfill and other disposal taxes should be set at a level that makes efficient recycling and composting competitive with mixed waste disposal. The waste industry has estimated the incremental cost of running kerbside recycling schemes at £10 per household, which (assuming an initial collection of 140kg per household annually) equates to £70 a tonne, and a similar amount could be assumed for organic collections. With existing costs of landfill-oriented waste management at £50-£60 a tonne, this suggests that the landfill tax that is set to rise to £15 a tonne by 2004 should be doubled in order to make recycling and composting financially 'competitive' with landfill.[94]

If a £30 landfill tax were to be in place by 2007, a five-year programme of transitional finance would be needed in the short and medium term, to fund the costs of converting to an intensive recycling system. To estimate these conversion costs, the Consortium of eleven Collection Authorities in Essex undertook a study into the five-year incremental cost of a 60% diversion programme for the waste system as a whole. There were four main conclusions:

- the net system cost declined over time, in line with the experience of recycling as a declining cost industry;

- the bulk of capital costs could be covered through either private sector investment or leasing. The main need was for working capital to fund the deficits over and above the council's current waste budgets;

- the system costs were sensitive to the speed at which the residual rounds could be reduced, and to the range of savings discussed above in the section on smart recycling;[95]

- the aggregate transition funding requirement for a 60% diversion programme for all Essex is £40 million in revenue funds over five years, assuming all capital is privately financed. Of this, £22 million would cover the capital servicing costs and £18 million the working capital requirements of the collecting authorities.[96] This is equivalent to £8 million p.a. for a county of 615,000 households, and represents an increase of just under 50% on the existing collection authorities' spending on waste of £17 million p.a.[97].

Translated nationally and including the recycling credits transferred by the disposal authority, the Essex study suggests the need for conversion finance of £2.2 billion, or £440 million per year.[98]

(b) the sources of funds

There are four main sources from which the £2.2 billion could be raised:

(i) the landfill tax

The landfill tax should source £0.9 billion of the conversion programme, or 40% of the total. It could contribute in two ways:

- The landfill tax credit scheme should be radically revised, and the funds channelled through a body independent of the waste industry with its prime focus on the expansion of recycling.

Currently the landfill tax credit scheme has a potential yield of some £100 million p.a. This is likely to rise to £135 million p.a. by 2004. If £30 million were to remain for non-waste related projects, £70 million p.a. would be available to fund conversion. The sum would rise to £105 million p.a. by 2004, and – with an increase of landfill tax to £30 per tonne but falling landfill volumes – should average at least £100 million p.a. through to 2007. The target sum to be earmarked for intensive recycling should be set at £500 million over five years.

- £400 million should be earmarked from the revenues derived from an increase in the landfill tax above £15 a tonne, and from its extension to other forms of pre-treatment, for the completion of the conversion programme.

(ii) producer responsibility payments

- The Packaging Recovery Notes (PRN) system under the packaging regulations should be adapted to contribute at least £350 million to the municipal conversion programme over five years.

Since the inception of the PRN scheme in 1997, its contribution to the changes required in the municipal sector has been derisory. Even with the increased demand for municipal packaging to meet the 60% recycling target by 2006, the amount going to municipal recycling over four years is likely to be modest. The amount of packaging recyclate that the industry estimates it will need from municipal sources is 1.2 million tonnes p.a. by 2006. Were compliance schemes to pay the average municipal recycling cost of £70 a tonne, this would yield £84 million p.a. If, however, PRNs remain at their current average of some £21 a tonne, the level in 2005/6 will be only £25 million p.a., no more than a fifth of the total funds being contributed.

The total four-year sum going to local authorities at existing PRN prices would not exceed £100 million, out of a forecast £500 million to be paid in by the packaging-related firms, compared to an equivalent of £4.4 billion from their packaging counterparts in Germany.[99,100] Significant funds will continue to go to processors, either to finance low cost/low capture forms of recycling or as windfall gains.

The PRN system and its administration need to be changed. The following measures should be considered:

- raising packaging targets to the 80% level already achieved in Germany rather than the 60% figure for 2006 likely to be agreed in Brussels;

- establishing a PRN sales intermediary to provide greater co-ordination between the supply and demand of the compliance schemes, and to establish a guaranteed floor price for PRNs of £40 a tonne. Any operating deficit of the intermediary would be funded retrospectively by the compliance schemes;

- directing all processors to issue PRNs directly to suppliers of recyclate, at the same time requiring compliance schemes to purchase the PRN rights for municipally funded recyclates for at least 1 million tonnes up to 2004 and 2 million tonnes up to 2007 at a minimum of £40 a tonne.

These sums, amounting at least £320 million during the period to 2007, would be supplemented by similar arrangements under the producer responsibility directives due for introduction by 2006.

(iii) **direct government funding**

- Direct funding of £700 million over five years, or £140 million a year, should be contributed directly by central government.

This would include the current programmes:

- £140 million for recycling in 2002/3 and 2003/4;

- £220 million for PFI schemes up to 2003/4 (the PFI finance promotes capital intensive investment and long contracts; the remaining funds that have not been committed should be switched and added to the £140 million recycling programme);

- £50 million of New Opportunities finance for community-led recycling schemes.

These should be supplemented by support from Single Regeneration Budget (SRB) allocations, Public Service Agreements and a further tranche of programme finance in the next three-year spending review.

(iv) **local authorities**

Disposal authorities are already set to make a major contribution to recycling through the recycling credit scheme. They should not be required to contribute further. Some collection authorities also make significant contributions (in Essex in 1999/2000 the eleven consortium boroughs were already providing £1.6 million a year for recycling). Nevertheless:

- **unitary and collection authorities should take responsibility for contributing £250 million to the** conversion scheme from their share of the £1.127 billion allocation made in the current spending review, and or any similar allocation in the subsequent round

The government should ensure that this happens and if necessary issue the requisite guidance for the final two years of the current review period.

Conclusions on sourcing

There are already substantial waste-related funding flows circulating in the economy, all of which are set to expand. The landfill tax credit scheme and the packaging recovery arrangements have together generated some £750 million in the past five years, and the Government's current spending review was planned to inject a further £500 million over the three years up to 2003/4. This finance is substantially lower than that available in high performing recycling economies like Germany, but could have had a major impact if it had been used 'smartly'. This has not been the case. The funds have remained unco-ordinated, their control and use shaped more by concerns to increase commercialisation and limit public expenditure than by achieving a major shift to waste minimisation.

A five-year conversion programme to intensive recycling should not therefore be held back by lack of funds. What is required is a 're-wiring' of existing funds, and a clear direction be given for their use. This in turn would provide the context for a major programme of private investment – in all stages of the 'closed loop' economy – which government leadership on recycling has stimulated elsewhere.

4. Institutions

One of the developments in the field of industrial policy over the last decade has been a shift from the arguments about state versus markets, to the question of the design of institutions. The literature on successful long wave transitions from one industrial era to another has similarly moved beyond a primary emphasis on technology to focus on the interplay between new organisational paradigms and emerging technologies. Historically, the countries that have been able to develop appropriate organisational structures have been best able to capitalise on contemporary technological possibilities.

The economists' new interest in organisations cuts across the former poles of debate. It is no longer a question of the shift from the public to private sector (or vice versa), or from tax/grant-based economies to markets. It is rather an issue of the nature of the institutions in which markets are embedded, or that undertake public/non-market functions.

In the case of waste this poses a particular challenge. On the one hand it requires a state that can play a creative public role as long-term strategist, a setter of parameters and a guardian of public and environmental health. On the other it requires the opening out of the former waste sector to the knowledge industries and to the dynamic of the third 'social-market' sector, whose innovative ways of reconciling the market with social and economic goals are so pertinent to Zero Waste.

New governance

As far as the public functions are concerned, my argument is that there have been serious limitations to the neo-liberal model of government as it operated in the waste field in the 1990s. There are three institutional problems that need to be directly addressed:

- the relegation of the government function of strategic direction, and the redefinition of its role as market facilitator, has led to a subaltern culture in government. It is skilled in critical faculties and the management of meaning, and in the application of market analysis to external propositions. But it has been leached of know-how and strategic confidence, and has therefore failed to establish an autonomous public identity for a function that demands it;

- there has been a consequent fragmentation of policy and ineffectiveness of implementation;

- a large, Weberian, rule-based organisation (the Environment Agency) has been created to administer the entrepreneurial function of environmental protection and promotion of clean production.

What is needed is a new model of waste governance. This would build on the positive features thrown up by the innovations of the 1990s (the readiness to consult widely, to decentralise and to experiment) and the developments of the past two years.

Central Government

- The Policy and Innovation Unit in the Cabinet Office is in the best position to develop the long-term government strategy for intensive recycling which up to now has been so lacking. It needs to be complemented by two things: (a) resource innovation units in each of the principal Departments concerned with waste, staffed by specialists who understand the new paradigm – since their task is to help make it work – as well as those with direct experience of the new paradigm in practice; and (b) a small group of staff in the Central Delivery Unit to work with the resource innovation units from the Departments in implementing the strategy.

Local Government

- Waste Minimisation Boards should be created for each waste disposal area that would combine the strategic waste functions of collection and disposal authorities. The main task of the Board would be to advance Zero Waste within that area. Control of the bodies would rest primarily with the existing collection authorities, which would delegate the operational side of disposal to the present disposal authorities.

- The central government resource innovation units would form the core of a network of waste minimisation units attached to the Waste Minimisation Boards throughout the country.

'Disposal rights' to local community trusts

- A new model for the administration of disposal assets is required, based on the principle that the 'pollutee controls'. The waste disposal rights attached to sites with disposal facilities would be placed in the hands of local community trusts. The facilities would be managed under contract by specialist disposal companies, and jointly administered by the relevant local authority body and the trust.

The principal benefit of this arrangement would be that those most affected by the existence of a disposal facility would have ownership rights vested in them as custodians of health and environmental protection. They would enjoy the 'locational rent' generated by the planning permissions granted to particular sites, and would be required to use that rent to employ specialist technical advisers and finance an independent testing regime. They would also be able to invest in the betterment of the area affected by the facility. All liability for the sites would rest with the facility operator and the local authority.

The trusts should be elected by and report to the relevant parish councils. They should include on their council of trustees people with environmental knowledge whose role would be to contribute to the delivery of the environmental aims of the trust.

Granting ownership over waste disposal rights represents an internalisation of externalities which complements the principle of 'polluter pays'. In this case the internalisation is not restricted to the receipt by those subject to pollution of post-facto compensation payments (the 'pollutee paid'). It offers the pollutee the ability to reduce the dangers of pollution in the first place, through control of the terms of operation and monitoring of practices.

The Environment Agency

- The planning, protection and enforcement functions of the Environment Agency with respect to waste need to be redefined and re-organised;[101]

- the function of providing IPPC certification for new and expanded facilities should be subject to greater public scrutiny by introducing a 'call-in' mechanism and provision for third party appeal;

- the monitoring of facilities should be undertaken by a strengthened inspection and testing service, whose terms of service should preclude it from later working for companies for which it had the responsibility of inspection;

- the prosecution function should be spun off as a stand-alone Environmental Prosecution Service to which both the EA inspection service and the neighbourhood trusts could submit evidence;

- the Environment Agency should extend its remit to include an advisory function on pollution control and waste minimisation innovations.

Intermediary institutions for Zero Waste markets

In addition to institutions to promote clean production, there are four functions that have to be fulfilled in facilitating the conversion to a Zero Waste paradigm:

- market development

- systems know-how

- a re-oriented profession

- financial intermediaries

The nature of the new waste system that is established will depend on which institutions perform these functions and how far they are open to the kinds of knowledge and social economy on which Zero Waste depends.

Market development

The first of the functions is now being undertaken by WRAP, a not-for-distributed-profit company limited by guarantee, set up in late 2000, and already providing a level of leadership in market development which had been absent from either the public or private sectors. WRAP has rightly given priority to exploring uses and markets for compost including the establishment of standards, and is in the process of allocating seed funds for a substantial expansion of newsprint capacity by tender.

Developing the supply side

WRAP represents the demand side of the new recycling. It is on the supply side that new initiatives are needed. There is still a serious shortage of know-how in both recycling and composting, in a field which also calls for the new ways of working outlined in Chapter Four. The large waste companies have had difficulty in entering this field effectively, relying as they do on traditional collection techniques and capital-intensive sorting and processing. The highest recycling and diversion rates have been achieved by the community sector and by creative council officers working with Direct Services Organisations (DSOs).

Yet their numbers are still limited, and their resources restricted. The community sector has been successful in areas such as social marketing, the development of new types of collection vehicle, the reskilling of collectors, waste composition analysis, local composting, joint materials marketing and the publication of an excellent new journal. They are, however, with one exception, still relatively small organisations, working with limited finance and not yet with the capacity to offer a full four-stream Zero Waste service for any district or borough. Similarly, the innovative councils and their DSOs are necessarily confined to their own boundaries and operate within the local authority financial restrictions. Neither of them yet constitutes a developed supply side for the extension of smart recycling throughout the country.

A new intermediary institution is needed to develop the supply side in the same way that WRAP is developing demand. In many jurisdictions abroad this role has been played by an animating agency. The customary functions are the development of operating manuals, of recycling software and management information systems, of social marketing materials, technological search and training. They play a role similar to that of the 'real service centres' in the industrial districts of Italy and Spain, providing a range of information, strategic planning, training and advice to small firms, similar to that supplied internally in large firms by central service departments. In the UK context this would be part of the job description of a Zero Waste Agency.

Investment finance

There is also a question of finance. The 'new wave' recyclers have not attracted finance from the conventional banking network, partly because of a low asset base (in the case of the community sector) or because of statutory restrictions on borrowing (in the case of local authorities).

Nor has recycling been seen as a bankable proposition, as compared to a large disposal contract with guaranteed gate fees over 25 years. Instead, community and Direct Services Organisation (DSO) recycling has grown on the basis of working capital advanced by client councils, supplemented by grants. Grant funding rather than private investment has been the rule for the expansion of municipal recycling.

This remains an option for the kind of conversion programme outlined above. The funds realised from central government or the landfill tax could be granted directly, or through an intermediary institution such as a

Zero Waste Agency. The latter has the advantage that the grant giving is undertaken by those with knowledge of the sector, and can be supported with other intangible services. Innovation is further stimulated if grants of this kind are administered through flexible bidding systems, in conjunction with specialist advice provided to applicants, and specialist adjudicators.[102]

An alternative option would be to shift the bulk of available funds away from grants to investment. The rationale for this approach is that in the long run intensive recycling should reduce council waste budgets as in the leading North American municipalities. If this is the case, and if service fees paid by municipalities for integrated collection services are held at current budgetary levels, then there is money to be made. The market for waste management services should be structured so that recycling and composting remain economically attractive for municipalities while providing a positive rate of return to the service provider. In this case intensive recycling becomes bankable.

Social venture capital

The investment approach opens up a new range of possibilities for the technical support and finance of intensive recycling. Because of the economic uncertainties of a new sector and the long payback period, a transitional institution is needed based on the model of social venture capital and development banking. It would be set up, like WRAP, as a company limited by guarantee. Its task would be to promote social enterprises to undertake inregrated, recycling-led collection systems, working in the first instance with client local authorities to expand existing enterprises or to promote new ones that would draw together on their boards and in their management the many skills and cultures required.

In some instances the new enterprise might be a joint venture between an existing community recycler, a DSO and an overseas established recycler. In others it might be a subsidiary of an existing waste company in conjunction with the community sector. Or the interest of a range of suppliers might prompt a local authority to break up a borough wide contract into smaller areas for the suppliers to manage independently.

The financial package would have four features:

- the contract between the social enterprise ('the contractor') and the local authority would cover all aspects of waste management within the collection authority, to allow the full system economies of intensive recycling to be realised;

- the contractor would guarantee to provide a comprehensive service to the collection authority for the existing budgetary cost (in real terms) over a ten-year period;

- the contract would be based on partnership working, with the council contributing agreed resources (such as publicity, depot and bulking space, maintenance services and some working capital) as a condition for the contractor's financial guarantee;

- the social investment trust as the venture capital instrument would provide capital in the form of equity, preference shares, unsecured loans, and (for some types of expenditure) grants, and would also act as guarantor for the financial and performance package to the client authority.

The advantage of this arrangement is that it would remove financial risk and the transitional cost premium from the client authority – both of which have been such barriers to the expansion of recycling. With this on offer, the contractor would be in a position to negotiate use of council assets at a low marginal cost, and at the same time would be encouraged to adopt smart recycling techniques in order to minimise debt.

More generally, while the goals of both the social investment trust and the contracting enterprise would be the expansion of intensive recycling and regeneration, this would be subject to commercial constraints. As the experiences of the social enterprise sector indicate, the combination of social and environmental goals subject to trading disciplines encourages production efficiency. Whereas grant applicants tend to inflate costs in their applications, those receiving a loan have an interest in containing them. The investment model would build in a drive for innovation and efficiency that has often been lacking in grant based organisations.

Another relevant social enterprise lesson is that other investment can be attracted by the goals of the organisation rather than its profitability. The pressure on large corporations to observe a triple bottom line has meant that they are increasingly looking for well-managed outlets, which meet social and environmental criteria, for support or investment. Both the Zero Waste Investment Trusts and the new generation of recycling enterprises would be attractive to corporate and ethical investors from this perspective.

Initially a Zero Waste Investment Trust would be established nationally and used as an instrument for the placing of funds channelled from the Landfill Tax Credit Scheme and a reformulated Private Finance Initiative (PFI). It would form local trusts, aiming to attract onto their Boards leading entrepreneurs from the commercial and community sectors who have an environmental orientation. The Trusts – like good development banks – would employ technical specialists, as well as business and financial managers, to provide advice and support to the recycling enterprises and to the Trust's financial arm.

The overall advantage of this approach is that it would introduce an economic dynamic directed towards Zero Waste. It would not be dependent on a continuing flow of grant funding. Returns from the investments would be channelled back into an expansion of the project.

Although its initial focus would be on local authority recycling, it would be expected to diversify and invest in commercial and industrial recycling projects (which commonly have a much shorter payback than the municipal sector).

A supply side Investment Trust would have an interest in promoting training programmes for the management and operation of intensive recycling systems in its area, either as part of existing courses and institutions or as a stand-alone Zero Waste Academy. An Academy, like a specialist technical school on the continent, would combine teaching and research on the full range of Zero Waste issues, and act as a catalyst for these issues in other universities and colleges.

With WRAP promoting the demand side, and the Investment Trusts facilitating the supply, the UK would have the potential to implement a programme of conversion to intensive recycling which would be economic and innovative. This would provide a step change in the movement towards a Zero Waste economy.

X Beyond Recycling

I have argued that municipal waste is the first step for a Zero Waste policy. It is centred on householders, (who have a key role in the post-waste order as recyclers, voters and consumers) and local authorities (who are the local public interpreters of environmental imperatives). It is a segment of waste more open to direct government influence than other parts of the waste flow, and at the same time connects to small firms and local institutions and their waste practices via the municipal trade waste service.

But even a radical transformation of municipal waste policy can only take things so far. The next step is to promote increases in recycling and composting in the commercial, industrial, construction and agricultural spheres. Alongside that, policy has to reach back to promote reduction of waste in the first place. Recycling in this sense is only a staging post. It is new production processes, material substitution, materials efficiency and design for extended product life that will be necessary to carry Zero Waste further.[103]

One estimate of the relative impact of different Zero Waste measures on greenhouse gas (GHG) reduction has been made for Western Europe by the Delft Group using the Markal model. Table 8 presents its results based on several hundred case studies in the second half of the 1990s.[104] The Delft Group was not able to analyze product reuse and product substitution in any depth, and its recycling category (accounting for less than a sixth of potential reductions) is narrowly defined to refer primarily to plastics recycling.

What these results show, nonetheless, is the importance of moving beyond recycling. Recycling is part, but only a part, of a wider green materials revolution. As the 1998 USEPA study confirms, while there are major GHG savings to be made from recycling and composting, GHG reduction will always be greater if waste is prevented rather than managed.[105] The Delft research highlights the

Table 8   The significance of different elements of Zero Waste strategies to GHG emissions reduction

Design for Environment Strategies Emission reduction potential (MtCO2e)	
Increased feedstock efficiency (less energy intensive processes, reduced losses during materials production)	50 - 100
Increased material efficiency (high strength materials, new alloys, composites, improved quality control to reduce variations in materials quality, reduced waste of materials during production, higher design strength, less material intensive design, materials standardisation)	100 - 200
Increased product efficiency (such as new packaging concepts, car sharing, increased product life, multi functional products)	50 - 150
Materials recycling/energy recovery (mainly plastics recycling)	100 - 200
Product reuse (renovation of buildings, design for disassembly)	25 - 50
Feedstock substitution (biomass feedstocks for plastics, solvents, fibres)	50 - 100
Materials substitution (renewable materials, less CO2 intensive materials, materials with improved physical characteristics, recyclable materials, material innovations and substitution leading to emission reductions in the use phase of vehicles and buildings)	200 - 300
Product substitution (product service concepts, less material-intensive products, products requiring less maintenance, long life products)	100 - 200
Total	675 - 1300

Source: Gielen, Kram and Brezet (1999)

major savings that can be made from changes in the resources used in industry, the efficiency with which they are used, and the types of goods – their durability and level of performance – that are produced to service consumption needs.

Policies to promote the new green materials economy are more complex than those involved in the expansion of municipal recycling. The changes required are pervasive. They reach throughout the economy, covering multiple facets of production and consumption. They have necessarily to work with industry for it is the producers who have to introduce the new paradigm. Policy is therefore directed at re-shaping the terms under which the market operates in order to provide the framework, the incentives and the information to encourage change.

In addition to the traditional government instruments such as regulations, generalised tax breaks and standardised grant programmes, three innovative approaches to environmental policymaking have had relevance for the encouragement of waste minimisation and materials efficiency:

- extended producer responsibility;

- innovations in public finance;

- knowledge economy instruments.

Together these provide the means to speed up changes already underway.

1. Extended Producer Responsibility

The concept of private property has from its inception had to identify the rights of 'quiet enjoyment' conferred by ownership, and the limitations on the use of that property if it harms others. The principles of environmental liability and 'polluter pays' marketise the infringement of these limits, expressing damage in monetary terms so that it can be internalised in the accounts of the polluter.

This has been effective when pollution can be traced to an identified source, such as a large factory, and its impact quantified. But what if the pollution has multiple sources? Are the harmful effects of CFCs from a discarded refrigerator the responsibility of the manufacturers of CFCs, of the fridge maker, the retailer for selling it, or the user for discarding it? Who is responsible for the pollution caused by nappy waste – Proctor and Gamble for producing the disposables, or the baby for using them? For issues such as resource productivity and waste, there are many points of responsibility in any product chain. We can speak of the socialisation of responsibility.

Extended Producer Responsibility (EPR) addresses this problem in an original way. It shifts the focus away from production facilities to product systems and design. In the words of Gary Davis, a leading contributor to the ideas and practices of Clean Production:

"Extended Producer Responsibility as a broad principle states that producers of products bear a significant degree of responsibility for the environmental impacts of their products throughout the products' life cycles, including upstream impacts inherent in the selection of materials for the products, impacts from the manufacturer's production process itself, and downstream impacts from the use and disposal of the products. Producers accept their responsibility when they design their products to minimise the life-cycle environmental impacts and they accept legal, physical, economic or informational responsibility for the environmental impacts that cannot be eliminated by design."[106]

He then outlines a set of principles to use in applying EPR, which include the following:

- schemes should create effective feedback to product designers to stimulate clean production;

- they should take a life cycle approach and be directed at producing life cycle benefits;

- there should be a clearly defined locus of responsibility;

- policies should be tailored to specific product systems;

- they should increase communication between producers throughout the product chain;

- policies should stimulate innovation by concentrating on improved outcomes not processes;

- there should be means of assessing the environmental and economic results of the policy, particularly where schemes are voluntary;

- policy should be framed with stakeholder involvement.

From this it should be clear that EPR is a policy instrument that reaches right back into product design and to issues that are at the centre of any industrial Zero Waste Strategy. How directly it does so will depend on the design of any particular scheme and the target levels set.

In the case of the EU's Packaging Waste Directive, targets are primarily set in terms of recycling and recovery levels, but the fact that the cost of meeting these has to be paid for by those in the packaging chain means that there is an increased monetary incentive for each of them to reduce the amount of packaging and improve its recyclability. The impact of the Directive, and of earlier national packaging measures, is reflected in the technical changes that are already taking place in the packaging industry, partly through light-weighting and partly through the substitution of biodegradable materials.

The EU has taken the lead in reducing the quantity and hazardous nature of waste through sectoral Directives. It is requiring producers to take responsibility for meeting graduated recycling targets for batteries, end of life vehicles and electrical and electronic equipment, as well as adopting 'design for recycling' and the reduction or phaseout of heavy metals and other hazardous substances. The use of EPR to control and reduce hazardous waste in British Columbia is summarised in inset 5.

As an instrument, extended producer responsibility can be tailored to specific products and substances, it is flexible in its application, and encourages collective responsibility within a product chain for the environmental impact of that chain. It can be used to reduce or phase out a wide number of substances, and substitute them with alternatives, from chlorine based materials like PVC and solvents, to non biodegradable plastics and chemicals in babies' nappies.

In the UK, the government has relied primarily on encouraging voluntary producer responsibility arrangements. By the late 1990s schemes existed in vehicles, batteries, tyres, newspapers and electrical and electronic equipment, but in most of these cases the advances have been limited, and less effective in changing the course of the sector and developing new technologies than the legislative programmes on the continent.[108]

The one legislative scheme has been in packaging in response to the EU Directive. In this and other forthcoming Directive-led programmes, the principal question remains how to shift government policy from being a passive implementer of EU Directives (and in some cases a force for diluting their terms) to being a proactive promoter of EPR as a means of achieving environmental goals and of stimulating new technology. In practice, the dominant emphasis of UK policy in EPR, as in other waste-related directives, has been on minimising costs rather than on maximising environmental outcomes.

In this regard it is striking that the recent assessment of EPR in Packaging in the UK by DEFRA's Advisory Committee on Packaging began by stating that 'one of the key objectives for the UK has been to achieve its environmental targets at the lowest possible cost to industry', without any assessment of the environmental impact or the priorities that should be set in implementing the Directive. It was unclear at the time the report was written that the UK would meet its targets, which would anyway leave it 'below the level of many other Member States'. What the Committee was certain of was that the scheme had minimised the cost.

The report reflects all that is weakest in the 'old order' approach to recycling in the UK. It sets incineration in direct competition with recycling in its recommendations on targets, resisting the EU Commission's proposals to replace 'recovery' tonnages by recycling. It warns against any attempt by the Commission to reduce the amount of packaging, and against any attempt to introduce reuse rates, and argues against high targets for individual materials. Rather it proposes that glass is given priority over paper and cans since paper would involve kerbside collection and, like cans, would be a lighter material when the targets are set by weight. There is no mention of the relative contributions of each of these materials to resource conservation and GHG reduction, which is one of the prime purposes of the Directive in the first place.[109] The predomenantely corporate Task Force represents a product chain which is not taking full extended responsibility for its environmental effects.

Rather than this approach, the government should outline a programme of EPR which leads rather than follows EU Directives. This is the policy which has been followed so successfully in Germany, and to a lesser extent in Sweden and Holland, and which has placed those countries in the lead in new recycling and waste reduction technology. The programme should be developed out of the joint waste minimisation and materials efficiency initiatives discussed below, and cover products as well as materials that have been difficult to recycle or that cause hazards in disposal.

Inset 5

Producer Responsibility and Household Hazardous Waste in British Columbia

During the 1990s the Government of British Columbia targetted the removal of hazardous waste (accounting for 1%-2% of household waste) from residuals sent for disposal. Initially in 1990 they established 8 pilots depots for households to deposit hazardous items, but these were only partially successful and were later closed. They also provided recycling incentives for tyres and batteries, which led to the recycling of 20 million tyres and 5 million vehicle batteries between 1991/2-1998/9.

But from 1992 they adopted a producer responsibility approach, putting the onus on manufacturers to administer and fund the waste reduction programmes:

- Used lubricating oil. Sellers of oil either had to take back used oil at no charge or arrange for agents to accept it. Each year this diverts more than 40 million litres of used oil.

- Paint. Paint brand-owners were required to take responsibility for the safe disposal of used paint. They established a not for profit company to do so for paint, aerosols and empty containers. The company has 103 depots throughout the province, and is financed by a small eco fee per can, which is paid by producers. In four years they collected 11 million litres of paint. Oil based paints are shipped to hazardous treatment/disposal facilities; latex paints are recycled into construction products; paint cans go to steel mills; and some paint is re-used.

- Pharmaceuticals. In 1996 the industry established a voluntary stewardship programme, for hazardous drugs to be returned to 650 pharmacies for safe collection and disposal.

- Solvent/flammables, domestic pesticides, gasoline and pharmaceuticals. The Government required producers to establish stewardship programmes for waste products. They jointly opened 35 depots, financing them either by an eco fee or through producer subscription.

These schemes have to be independently audited. In some, such as paint, there are reuse and recycling targets. The long term aim is to encourage the switch by consumers and producers to less hazardous materials and products (from water based to oil based paints for example.)

2. Innovations in public finance

Green tax proposals aimed at encouraging the closed loop economy have focussed on raising taxes on material inputs and waste. We have already discussed waste taxes. At their current levels, they are not a significant enough cost for most industries to encourage a radical redesign of the product chain. Similarly, there is limited scope in the UK to pursue the proposals considered elsewhere for raw material charges and subsidy reduction, or virgin material import ceilings.

The exception is the construction sector, whose use of materials can be significantly influenced by taxes on primary aggregate and waste disposal. The tax of £2 a tonne on inert waste taken to landfill introduced in 1996 has led to a fall in landfilling of this class of waste by a third (more than 12 million tonnes) in the two years between 1997/8 and 1999/2000.[110] This has led to some increase in recycling, which will be reinforced by the introduction of an aggregates tax in 2002 at a level approaching 50% of the ex-works value of virgin stone.

For commercial and industrial producers, reliant on material imports and for most of whom waste costs are trivial, the measures that promise to have a significant effect on resource productivity are those introduced in Britain to reduce CO_2 within the context of the Kyoto targets. There are five elements here:

- the climate change levy (CCL), taxing electricity, gas and other non-renewable energy sources used by business;

- the exemptions to the levy granted to energy intensive businesses which sign energy efficiency agreements;

- the earmarking of part of the levy to finance a Carbon Trust to take the lead in energy efficiency (and waste reduction) advice and in low carbon innovation;

- the earmarking of another part of the levy to provide

capital allowances for energy saving technology;

- the provision of start-up finance for an emissions trading scheme, through which firms which have exceeded their CO2 emission reduction targets can sell the excess to those who have fallen short.

There are a number of innovations here: the primary resource tax, which partly reflects the carbon intensity of fuels; the use of tax explicitly to change business behaviour with the tax revenues hypothecated to further the same goals; the use of negotiated agreements with firms to change corporate behaviour in return for tax reductions; the establishment and funding of a not-for-profit Trust to act as an animator of innovation; and finally the marketisation of target performance through emissions trading. In the history of public finance this package would qualify for a chapter on innovative instruments. Many have been advocated by environmental economists, but few in the mid-1990s could have expected they would be introduced so rapidly.

The above measures have been put in place to increase energy efficiency. The question is how far they can be developed to improve material resource productivity. As the Dutch research suggests, the two are closely related and a major impact on energy reduction can be made through improved material productivity. It is not just a question of getting heavy energy users to improve their energy efficiency, but of changing manufacturing production so that it uses less of the energy-intensive primary materials and/or extends their life through reuse and recycling. This is the reason why Zero Waste is important for Climate Change policy.

There is a parallel here between pollution control and emissions reduction. The first stage in both is to cut down the emissions of the major polluting plants and processes. In each case, the plants and their emissions can be readily identified (and for this reason they are likely to be the early core of players in the emissions trading market). The challenge comes when the cause of the emissions cannot be ascribed to a single plant but to the product chain as a whole. Can the UK climate change measures be widened to take in such product chain issues and waste reduction/resource productivity more generally?

The question can be posed first in relation to emissions trading. For such trading to work, firms have to register current emission levels and agree targets for their reduction. There have been 44 agreements in the UK to date, and there is a view that the existing criteria of eligibility that allows firms to trade reduction targets for tax concessions should be widened. Under the likely terms of the international trade in permits, once a reduction target is agreed a firm (or country) will have the option to meet it by emissions reduction, sequestering carbon or by buying credits. As a result major GHG emitters in North America are already preparing for the new trading regime by investing in projects that will promote sequestration or large emissions reductions (such as forestry and agriculture) and hence offset their own shortfalls.

With respect to waste and materials, it should be possible in principle for firms, either individually or as a product chain pursuing the Design for Environment Strategies outlined in Table 8, to register their current CO_2 emission levels and reduction targets and to generate surplus certificates for sale. Given that the price of the certificates when they are internationally traded is forecast to be substantial, this would provide a major incentive for the adoption of industrial Zero Waste policies. The issue is whether the registration and target regime in the UK can take such policies into account. How could the benefits of substituting biodegradable plastics for oil-based plastics be included in the scheme; or the production of a fully recyclable car with a thirty-year lifespan?

Similar questions could be asked of other parts of the UK's fiscal package: could such material productivity initiatives be granted the Climate Change levy reductions in return for an agreement covering material efficiency as well as energy efficiency improvements? Could firms that provide lifelong guarantees on products with take-back agreements qualify for the extra capital allowances? Could those firms which agree to standardise components to ease remanufacture and repair receive funding from the Carbon Trust?

The answers to these questions must in principle be yes. Waste minimisation and materials efficiency agreements could be replicated on the model of those for energy efficiency, and indeed would overlap. But, as with the producer responsibility approach, the challenge comes when no one firm can make the necessary changes on its own. In such cases, the agreements and incentives need to be collective.

Instruments of the information economy

A third approach sees the generation, interpretation and distribution of information as the critical point of entry for Zero Waste policy. The starting point for any re-orientation of productive practices, it argues, is to make their current environmental impact visible. Where economists have sought to marketise environmental costs and benefits which have been hitherto outside the market, so in parallel the same thing needs to happen with environmental information, to make visible what has hitherto remained unseen.

In relation to Zero Waste this entails the qualitative and quantitative study of the impact of different types of product and productive system on the environment and an assessment of how they can be improved. In the past thirty years this has generated a wide range of new ways of looking at the material flows of the economy and their effects. (The ex post quantification of material flows is one example, along with life cycle analysis and dynamic ex ante estimates of flows and processes to judge the impact of alternative paths of technical change.) It has also generated new ways of counting (through the development of environmental reporting and performance indicators) and a new level of scientific testing of hazardous effects.

For some writers the project of increased environmental knowledge is parallel to that of increased social knowledge which accompanied the expansion of government social policy in the nineteenth century, with its extended apparatus of statistics, inquiries, inspectorates and institutional controls.[111] For others it represents an endless task of trying to control (carry on business in spite of) the uncontrollable effects of modern technology, where each new attempt produces its own hazards.[112] Much of the debate has centred on the identification of risk and how its potential impacts are assessed and distributed.[113] For all these writers the role of science and information about the environment has become the pivotal point of environmental politics. It is also the starting point of any project of ecological modernisation. In this context government policy towards the production of information, its interpretation and circulation becomes the critical instrument for environmental reform.[114]

This informational economy feeds into the process of Zero Waste production in six ways:

- as the stimulus for action by civil society;

- as the basis for subsequent development of government policy and regulation;

- as an input for ecodesign and new environmental technologies;

- as productive information for re-oriented producer strategies and practices;

- as a source of data for public monitoring and surveillance;

- as information to consumers to inform purchasing decisions.

These represent the political, governmental and economic dimensions of environmental transition and each can be strengthened through government support.

A starting point for considering a policy on information and Zero Waste are the conclusions of the Cabinet Office report on Resource Productivity. Although the report raises the possibility of extending the principles of environmental taxation to the field of materials, its prime recommendations reflect the knowledge economy approach. The list of recommendations includes the following: the development of Material Flows Analysis and environmental accounts, further research on the role of natural resources in the economy and the barriers to improved resource productivity, the development of resource productivity proxies and measurements, an assessment of existing information providing bodies (and by implication a strengthening of the function), a programme of awareness-raising around resource productivity issues, an extension of environmental reporting by major companies, a connection of sustainability issues across departments and their internalisation into Treasury assessments, possible indicative targets, and support of conversion initiatives through advice, finance, public procurement and improved training and education.[115]

These are all necessary elements for a new resource productivity policy, but as a programme they need more specificity and scope. The impact on waste minimisation of the proposals for self-monitoring through the publication of environmental reports, for example, will depend on the nature of the reporting: what is covered, how far it extends into the issues covered in Design for the Environment and so on. As we noted earlier there is pressure for environmental reporting from insurance companies and pension funds, which have an interest in the real progress being made rather than its presentation. Thus, much rests on the degree to which the format and substance of reporting reflects the wider perspectives of Zero Waste.[116]

Self-reporting needs to be supplemented by enhanced rights and resources for independent environmental auditing bodies, and by schemes such as eco-labelling, or the successful environmental league tables in Indonesia in which a ranking of the environmental performance of major firms is published, with those at the bottom given notice before publication to provide them with an opportunity for improvement. In an era when major companies are more than ever dependent on the integrity of their brands, the opening of the environmental books becomes a powerful policy lever that works through the market, via the impact of both green consumers and ethical investors.

Secondly, the data on industrial and commercial waste needs to be regularised and extended. Waste Strategy 2000 set a target of a 15% reduction on 1998 levels for commercial and industrial waste going to landfill by 2005, which is some five million tonnes. The way in which this might be measured is by data from landfills, but this does not allow the targets to be made firm or sector specific. As far as data on the latter is concerned, the Environment Agency carried out a National Waste Production Survey of 20,000 firms in 1998, the first of its kind for many years. But this is not being repeated, it is said, because of a shortage of finance. Yet it has to be recognised that information of this kind is as critical for effective policy and industrial change in this field as it is in the macro control of the economy.

Thirdly, the proposals for further research and for technological support need to be brought together and responsibility for them placed in a Clean Production Centre. This is an idea proposed by the OECD and implemented in a number of OECD member countries. The main purpose of such centres is to act as an entrepreneurial driver of the new materials policy. The Centre would promote clean production research, design for the environment initiatives, and the extension of Zero Waste advisory services, and in particular would:

- undertake and/or sponsor sectoral, material and process specific research;

- provide a link between independent research institutes and firms on the model of the successful Steinbeis foundation in Germany;

- produce manuals and provide advice on waste reduction, feedstock substitution and materials efficiency;

- supply relevant market and technical information to small and medium firms.

Above all it would be charged, like the Carbon Trust, with animating change."[117]

One option would be to attach it to the Carbon Trust, whose terms of reference already include advice on waste reduction. As we have seen there is a strong interconnection between advice on energy, water and waste reduction, and between their effects. The scope and resources of the trust could be expanded to take in the promotion of innovations for increased materials productivity as well as energy efficiency.

Even if established separately the trust should remain closely linked to the Carbon Trust (and to WRAP) and would be funded in a similar way with resources drawn from the Climate Change levy and from increments in the landfill/disposal tax.

A policy package

The three approaches outlined here are not alternatives. Nor are they mutually exclusive. Each provides an innovative entry point for policies that promote the changes necessary for Zero Waste. They also provide a range of instruments, which largely complement each other, and which can be further linked to more established policy tools such as regulations and public purchasing. As can be seen in the case of energy efficiency, once the goals are clear, a variety of tools can be drawn on to change the course of production and the nature of innovation in any industry.

The central point again, as in the case of municipal waste, is a clarity about goals. There may be strengthening independent pressures upon the corporate world to improve environmental performance, but these need to be contextualised within a clear government perspective. The government alone can provide leadership and purpose on issues that span the range of particular interests.

Business itself recognises this. The Advisory Committee on Business and the Environment gave priority to its recommendation that: 'government makes clear to business the broader goal of resource productivity in its policies on waste minimisation and reducing waste to landfill'.[118] The role is one of intellectual and policy leadership.

In the case of energy and climate change the ground has been well set, and the work of translating it into immediate policy was undertaken by a small task force led by Lord Marshall.[119] In the case of materials productivity and materials substitution, the new perspectives are less widely known.

- **The government should establish a Design for the Environment Commission.**

The Commission should identify the potential of these innovations in the UK context, draw up a programme for conversion, establish a set of targets and develop the policies needed to achieve them. The Commission would be made up of leading international specialists in the field of the green materials economy together with their equivalents in the UK. Their report should set out the new paradigm of green production. The policies to promote it should provide the incentives and make the sources of advice and information available for those who choose to pursue the approach. A report of this kind would provide the basis for synthesising the work of government and industry in this field.

This is a first step. At the same time, an immediate start

should be made on extending the idea of industry agreements introduced as part of the Climate Change levy. In this instance the agreements should not be negotiated solely with firms, but with groups of firms engaged in a particular product chain or production of materials.

One initiative of this kind which has been in operation for more than a decade is taking place in Holland. In 1989 the Dutch Parliament established a waste minimisation target of 10% by 2000 which was applied (flexibly) to 29 priority waste streams. For each of the streams, waste minimisation plans were drawn up through consultation between industry and government, and these were then translated into individual company environmental plans. The sectoral plans were embodied in covenant agreements between the industries and the government, and all companies in the sector or chain were issued with a handbook setting out the goals of covenant and a list of possible minimisation measures. Headway was made most rapidly with sectors which already had integral environmental tasks, such as the chemical industry, paper and paper goods and the dairy industry, but the work was then extended to other groups.[120]

Processes of this kind are already taking place in the UK around producer responsibility programmes, but there is a strong case for widening their scope and extending them to other sectors within the framework of national waste reduction targets. In particular sectoral working groups should consider how actions taken in the field of materials efficiency, product performance, product life extension and feedstock substitution could be linked to the CO2 reduction targets and future emissions trading.

National and local

The emphasis of industrial Zero Waste policy has been on actions to be taken by national government. But within a new policy framework there is much that local and regional government can also do. The national Clean Production Centre should be established with a network of regional sub-centres. Local and regional government, and the regional development agencies, can play a role as a link between existing environmental research institutions and local industry. There is scope for using public purchasing to encourage Zero Waste companies, and to work with them and other institutions on local reuse and CO_2 reduction schemes.[121] Above all, they can use their central information and material role as recyclers and disposers of municipal waste, to connect into the wider project of Zero Waste.

XI Conclusion

The environmental critique of modern production has advanced on two fronts: sources and sinks. One has highlighted industrialism's devastation of certain natural resources and ecosystems, the other the pervasive pollution from its wastes. There have been attempts in each case to provide remedies in isolation: to develop sustainable forestry at one end, for example, or to install pollution control equipment at the other. Both have had an impact – but both find themselves holding back the growing demands for new resources, and the growing quantity of wastes, as a sea wall holds back the pressures of a rising tide.

If the relentless growth of global material production is to be outpaced, the problems of sources and of sinks cannot be solved in isolation. They have to be seen as parts of a wider chain of production and consumption that must be reconfigured as a whole. The issue is one of changes in productive systems – how products and processes are designed, how they operate and how products and materials, once used, return again to the circuit of production.

The major transformation now being demanded in agriculture, where intensive farming is both depleting the soil and leaving residues – whether in the area of nitrogenous run-off or toxic middens – illustrates the point, as do the shifts taking place in the energy sector and in transport. In each case, the critique has broadened from an identification of particular environmental problems to a challenge to the economic architecture of the productive system as a whole. Whether for food, power or mobility the movement for reform is now being framed in terms of how needs are being met – and how they could be met differently in ways which would work with the grain of social and natural ecosystems rather than against them.

Beyond the waste ghetto

Zero Waste should be seen in this light. Much has been done since the early 1970s to reduce the pollution stemming from waste disposal and to encourage the reduction of waste. Yet the volume of waste and the problems resulting from it have continued to increase. This is how Joke Waller-Hunter, the OECD's Director of the Environment put it in 1999:

"Despite nearly 30 years of environmental and waste policy efforts in OECD countries, the OECD-wide increase in waste generation is still in 1:1 proportion to economic growth. A 40% increase in OECD GDP since 1980 has been accompanied by a 40% increase in municipal waste during the same period ...Consumer spending also follows these trends. According to our colleagues in the Economics Directorate, there is expected to be a 70%-100% increase in GDP by the year 2020 in the OECD area. I would personally not like to imagine a world where municipal waste generation is also 70%-100% higher than the already high levels of today".[122]

What was initially conceived as a confined policy problem had by the late 1990s become a gathering environmental nightmare, which led to waste being named as one of the 'red light' issues in the OECD's Environment Strategy in 2001.[123]

The first policy focus has been to improve the safety of the waste disposal sinks, the second to reconnect waste to industrial production through recycling. These have both been advanced from the end of the pipe – through the conduct of waste management. Yet, in Britain at least, the connections between recycling and the processing industries have been weak. Municipal recycling has been treated first and foremost as an 'option' for waste management. Its main perceived significance has been as a means of reducing the quantities of waste for disposal rather than providing high quality feedstock for industry. Only now, with the establishment of WRAP, are the connections between the recyclers and industry being systematically constructed so that the market for materials becomes not a problem but a raison d'être of municipal recycling.

'Low road' recycling has always faced difficulties as long as it remained primarily a waste disposal option. The various attempts to recycle or compost mixed waste have been gradually abandoned, in favour of a policy of source separation. Once waste materials are examined separately, the problems of quality and marketability are continually posed. What is the market for municipal compost if it contains high herbicide residues in garden waste, or contaminated meat in putrescible scraps? What is the value of plastic lined steel cans and plastic composites? What is it in the construction of a toaster that makes it difficult to repair? What are the economics of glass and plastic bottles that makes the industry so reluctant to reuse?

In each case, waste managers may conclude that the materials are unrecyclable, or that it makes no economic or even environmental sense to do so. But the problems of disposal push the question back on the table and pose it the other way round, namely: what would be required to make such a material technically and economically recyclable? Such a question takes waste managers beyond the end-of-pipe boundaries. It leads necessarily to questions about waste production, and waste production in turn leads on to issues of industrial design and manufacturing processes.

This is the first connection. The second is that between recycling and the other great arena of environmental concern – the sustainability of resources. Composting comes to be recognised as important not simply as a means of diverting bio-degradable waste from landfill, but of contributing to soil restoration and the fight against desertification. Or take paper. Recycling one tonne of waste paper preserves 17 trees. A modern recycling mill therefore saves five million trees a year. That is a measure of the importance of recycling. It shows how the problems of sinks and sources are linked and how they both, in their own way, flow into the wider questions of production.

The argument of this book is that waste cannot be treated in isolation. Attempts to do this whether using old or new technologies are necessarily limited for three reasons: first, the landfilling and incineration of mixed waste has been unable to eliminate the hazards associated with each. They can confine and attempt to manage them, but as regulations tighten, costs increase and the problems of everyday operation – of accidents, fires, malpractice, material failure, seepage and the scattering of toxic residues to air and water – continue to reappear.

Secondly, the disposal of waste removes materials from their cycle. Modern forms of disposal and pre-treatment are designed to generate some energy or material from the waste stream they deal with. Landfills produce harvestable bio-gas. Incinerators generate energy and extract low grade metal from their ash. Mixed waste composting produces a grey compost high in heavy metals which is sometimes used for landfill cover or land reclamation.But these represent no more than the salvage of resources during a process of destruction and bear no comparison with the resource savings from source separated recycling and composting.

Thirdly, restricting the problem of waste to that of its disposal is to sacrifice its role in the environmental transformation of industrial production. Landfills and incinerators ask no questions. They take what comes to them. They are driven by the requirement to operate within regulations at least cost. There are few prizes given for the cleanest landfill or the lowest emission incinerator. They have no incentive to hunt out the batteries in a consignment of mixed waste. If a load of PVC arrives at an incinerator, the issue is how to phase in its combustion in order not to exceed emission limits, rather than whether or not to divert it elsewhere. Far from having an interest in reducing hazards, disposers stand to benefit from them, hazardous and clinical waste disposal being at the top of the waste price hierarchy.

Much the same can be said of 'low road' recycling,

whether its aim is to divert from landfill or to meet government targets. It, too, is passive. Its dynamic is not to connect back to the industrial circuit to recover high value material or pre-empt toxic waste. Rather the effort is put into contesting regulations, and once they are set, into finding ways to meet their formal requirements at least cost. In this context a target or regulation is seen as a burden, not as an invitation to innovate.

Zero Waste has a different perspective. Waste is a sign of failure of industrial design. It is a symptom of wider issues. While waste has to be managed, the aim of Zero Waste is prevention, and the development of circuits that slow down the entropy of energy and materials and enhance nature's metabolic process. As Michael Braungart remarks, waste must equal food:

"The amount of organic waste produced by ants is more than four times higher than that produced by the six billion people in the world. But ants are not an ecological problem – they return all products of metabolism to various cycles. Nature knows no waste. All products of metabolism are recycled as 'food' for other organisms."[124]

Zero Waste seeks to understand why these circuits have broken down and how they can be restored. Whereas traditional waste management was geared to making waste invisible, Zero Waste aims to increase its visibility. Recyclers undertake waste audits and follow material flows. When they collect, instead of the closed wheeled bin, they use open plastic boxes. Instead of black bags, the new Italian collection systems provide transparent bags for food waste and residuals. The civic amenity sites (and in New Zealand many of the landfills) are no longer organised as inaccessible places for disposal, but as reception centres for recycling, reuse and repair – extensions of the car boot sale. The last few years have seen the reclamation of waste as a source of education and entertainment. Schools establish wormeries and include waste in their curricula. Communities ask for transparency in the monitoring of waste facilities and finance their own testing. Never has waste been so closely inspected, watched, tested and discussed.

The reason for this renewed visibility is so that all those involved in producing and handling waste can distinguish those parts of it that can be returned to production, from those parts which should not have been produced in the first place. I have argued that one of the important things about waste is that it is a vantage point for assessing the sustainability of modern industrial processes. Waste and its management serve as a stage of quality control for the whole system, tracing back defects (bad waste) to their source. To confine waste management to disposal or to passive recycling is to neglect its role as a point of innovation for clean production.

A similar point applies to waste management's new role as a link in the biological and technical circuits. It is no longer a terminus but a critical interchange in the process of material circulation. As such it needs to be integrated with the producers of waste on the one hand, and the users of the reclaimed materials on the other. Modern recycling no longer acts solely as collector and merchant, but as an active player in the system of knowledge production. Its starting point may be the channelling of unwanted material back into useful production, but it then acts as a promoter of new uses for old materials and of new materials (and products), both of which serve to increase the resource productivity of the system as a whole.

The most innovatory institutions in the new waste management have played this intermediary role, with engineers, material specialists and market researchers working alongside local industry on secondary material use. They have combined technical advice and research and advised regulators on new standards. In parallel, producer responsibility legislation encourages industries to assume these functions on their own behalf – sub-contracting the collection and sorting function – while undertaking their own programme of research and re-design to improve the life cycle of products and materials.

Zero Waste is not simply a form of waste management. It is a programme for innovation and industrial transformation. The construction of an incinerator or any of its chemico-energy variants undercuts this dynamic. It rests on the proposition that waste can be dealt with on its own terms, without venturing into the territory of how it is produced, or how materials could be reused most effectively. It poses its own set of questions – to do with economies of scale and how to control pollution – and maps its own political territory (covering planning permissions, local opposition and the terms and enforcement of regulations). It is inward looking, defending its interest politically against external pressures, rather than outward looking with a focus on wider industrial change.

As a result, while the construction of a new incinerator claims to answer some immediate issues of waste disposal, it sidesteps the association, in Waller-Hunter's words, 'between waste generation and climate change, deforestation, toxic substance releases, biodiversity loss, increased soil erosion and other problems.'[125]

It also fails to connect to the social and economic potential of Zero Waste. Waste prevention and recycling offer scope for local and regional industrialisation, urban regeneration, a range of 'green collar' jobs, and a means of improving environmental equity. One of Walter Stahel's main points is that lengthening product life entails a major substitution of labour for energy and materials, requiring as it does the development of regional repair workshops and the development of local loops for dematerialised fashion goods, and the taking back of goods for remanufacturing.[126]

Productive systems

Through waste, as through the pressures on natural resources, the environmental imperatives have forced a redefinition of the categories used to analyse the economy. Instead of the segmentation of linear production – primary materials, manufacturing, distribution, consumption and waste — environmental economists distinguish between different productive systems. They classify by sector or by material or social need, within a wider environmental system, and speak of an industrial metabolism and of material circuits, rather than the monetary flows of macro economic analysis.[127]

Zero Waste is therefore at root a productive systems perspective. As such it deals with complexity and multiple connections. It is also centrally about change. In terms of economic thought it speaks the language of Schumpeter rather than Smith, of destruction and innovation rather than market equilibrium. In its mainstream form, its analytical dynamic comes from the tension between the material demands of modern industrial production and the ecological limits of the natural world. Out of this tension comes the problematic of alternatives. Zero Waste is about different paths of development of productive systems.

New approach to policy

I have suggested that Zero Waste also involves a new approach to policy. This is necessary for three reasons. First, attempts by a central body — whether state or corporation — to manage a complex system by means of traditional forms of centralised command and control are bound to fail. As corporations have grown they have faced this core organisational problem, and the history of the current industrial era is one of experiments in organisation which combine decentralisation and synthesis in a way that allows innovation to flourish. States have faced a similar problem, one that is at the centre of discussions on the shape of a new regime for waste.

Secondly, waste and the green materials revolution pose questions of interdependence that cannot simply be solved by market instruments based on individualised property and responsibility. As Ulrich Beck puts it, technology has advanced to the point where individualised liability breaks down. This is true both of environmental effects and of changes in productive systems that are needed to minimise these effects. Policy therefore has to find new ways of dealing with socialised responsibility and interdependent production.

Third, the reduction in waste and changes in material production – because of their systemic character – have multiple impacts which demand a rewiring of traditional departments of the state. Joined up government is a way of talking about the need for new means for governing productive systems. An initiative may not meet the economic criteria in terms of the desired outcomes of a single department, but would pay its way if multiple outcomes were taken into account. Zero Waste produces multiple dividends, and this poses a challenge to existing structures and forms of assessment within government.

The discussion of British policy has explored some of the issues and innovations in the instruments of government in relation to waste and materials productivity, with the following conclusions:

- there is a central place in modern environmental policy for government leadership and a clear vision of the long term alternative. This provides the synthesis of perspective which is necessary for systemic change. Without it both government and industry will fragment into particularistic policies;

- producer responsibility is an innovative way of dealing with interdependence. Policy identifies groups of actors – in this case firms in a product chain – who can be collectively held responsible for a set of environmental effects, and asks them to develop alternative solutions. Government sets the parameters and targets and the group of actors decides how to meet them;

- fiscal policy can be used to support the process of environmental transition by recycling funds through hypothecation, or other tax/benefit packages, from one set of practices (or actors) to another. to another.

- Central government intervenes in the process of these financial flows, and may negotiate directly with large firms or groups of firms as to the terms on which the financial benefits are forthcoming. The energy efficiency agreements are an example of this and instruments of this kind could have wide ranging application in the field of materials and municipal waste, in the latter case through an expansion of public service agreements. They are a form of collective contract or, as the Dutch put it, a covenant;

- considering the conversion of industry towards Zero Waste through the lens of the knowledge economy places information and its circulation at the heart of new systems of government. How information flows within the system, particularly to those governing the system from the centre (whether government, industry or civil society) becomes a central issue, as do the sources of knowledge of those with responsibility for production (from households which compost, to large scale manufacturers). Zero Waste is information-intensive both as a system of production and a system of government;

- a key role is played by institutions that mediate between the three main spheres of the economy – the private market, the state and the household. These may be non profit companies carrying through entrepreneurial public functions on behalf of the government (as in the case of WRAP or the Carbon Trust), or community recyclers working at the interface between households, local government and material markets. The new form of governance has a central role for the third sector;

- finally there is the issue of the role of the market and regulation. My conclusion here is twofold. First markets and regulations are not alternatives. They are inter-dependent. The issue is not market versus regulation, but what kind of market and what kind of regulation. Second, Zero Waste requires more of both;

on the one hand a greatly expanded use of market instruments adjusted to provide the necessary incentives; on the other a strong environmental state to provide direction, to structure the market and administer a limited range of regulations. The market cannot do these things on its own.

As far as waste in the UK is concerned, the post neo-liberal period in the 1990s simultaneously weakened government in a sphere of environmental policy that required strong public leadership, and failed to structure a system of incentives which would encourage markets to work towards ends that were commonly agreed. This is the reason why British waste policy has failed in its own terms, and has left the UK so far behind in the progress towards a waste minimising economy.[128]

At the same time a range of policy instruments were developed, which, if reformulated, have the potential to create the economic climate, the incentives, the intermediary institutions and the social knowledge necessary for the programme of conversion which Zero Waste entails.

I have suggested that there are multiple outcomes from Zero Waste. There are also multiple paths towards it. An immediate one is the recycling and composting of municipal waste. The targets for this should be set high, both because of the urgency of the environmental issues at stake, and in order to focus the attention of all those engaged in municipal waste management on the central issues of transition. But industry itself should advance in parallel. It, too, should have ambitious targets, not just for each firm individually, but for the product chains of which they form a part.

For all those engaged in this work, Zero Waste should be understood, in a pragmatic sense, both as a target and a methodology. But it also represents a wider project - the redesigning of the system of industrial production and consumption to meet the imperatives and desires of a post-industrial age.

Endnotes

[1] For a brief summary of the scientific evidence, see P.Montague, 'Landfills are Dangerous', Rachel's Environment and Health Weekly no 617, 24th September 1998. This includes British cases.

[2] P.Elliott et al, British Medical Journal, August 17th 2001 and the Department of Health website. This study was commissioned in 1998 after the results of a major European study which looked at 21 sites, 10 of them in the UK, and found an increase of foetal malformation for women living within 3 km of a landfill site. Other UK government studies are now attempting to measure the air emissions and leachates from landfill sites.

[3] M.Ritter and B.Gugele, 'Annual European Community Greenhouse Gas Inventory 1990-1999', European Environment Agency April 2001.

[4] 'NIMBY' is an acronym for 'not in my back yard'.

[5] Among recent major campaigns against landfills in the UK, particularly notable have been those preventing the expansion of major landfill sites in Belfast, Cornwall, Kent and West Lancashire, and the closure of the Nant-y-Gwyddon landfill in the Rhondda.

[6] For Europe see European Environment Agency, 'Environment in the European Union at the turn of the Century', Copenhagen 1999 and J.Schmid, A.Elser, R.Strobel, M.Crowe, 'Dangerous Substances in Waste', Technical Report no 38, European Environment Agency, February 2000.

[7] A good recent survey of the scientific evidence on incinerators and pollution can be found in: M.Allsopp, P.Costner and P.Johnston, 'Incineration and Human Health', Greenpeace 2001.

[8] In the case of the largest UK incinerator, at Edmonton in North London, it was found that highly toxic mixed fly ash and bottom ash was being landfilled in Essex, stored in open heaps in East London, and used for road construction and as housing materials. Tests of the East London heaps found dioxin levels ranging from 241 to 946 nanogrammes (ng) per kg, in line with the 735 ng per kg level established by the incinerator operator in its mixed ash, and well in excess of the 50 ng per kg levels judged acceptable by Germany for ash levels in soil or public places such as children's playgrounds. Even higher levels were found in samples from the 44 allotments on which 2,000 tonnes of ash had been deposited from the Newcastle incinerator at Byker, in one case the level reaching 9,500 ng per kg. The Byker tests also found high lead

contamination, with 19 of the allotments tested showing levels above those (331 milligrammes per kg) that led to closure of the nearby City Farm. In the light of the findings from Edmonton and Byker, the Environment Agency launched an investigation into the fate of ash from all 11 municipal incinerators.

[9] Among UK plants that have been shut for reasons of fire and explosion in recent years have been the municipal incinerator in Dundee, and SITA's tyre incinerator in Wolverhampton. On the Wolverhampton plant see the ENDS Report no. 313, February 2001.

[10] The Edmonton incinerator, which was upgraded in 1996, registered nearly 1,800 exceedances with the Environment Agency between 1996 and 2000, exceedances being defined as emissions of 150% over the legal limit for at least an hour. It was only prosecuted once.

[11] The controversy over the operation of the Byker plant and its residues is only one of many waste scandals to have occurred internationally in the 1990s, in spite of modern regulatory structures being in place. In the case of Byker, the problems of ash contamination were first raised by the local allotment holders who funded their own tests, and together with the trade union at the plant, have had to engage in an 18-month dispute over the conduct, results and interpretation of official tests and the action stemming from them. This has culminated in a two-month 'citizen's inquiry', chaired by Andrew Bennett M.P., that has widened the issue into an investigation of Newcastle City Council's waste management strategy and the alternatives. On the centrality of contested science and information in contemporary environmental politics see Ulrich Beck, Ecological Politics in an Age of Risk, Polity Press, 1995.

[12] A survey of 4,000 UK landfill sites in 1993 found that 230 had suffered a major pollution incident, one third of them being modern 'containment' sites, and 10 of them having been started after 1990. 'The Waste Manager', March 20th-22nd 1994, cited in Williams P.T, Waste Treatment and Disposal, Wiley 1998 p.267.

[13] US Environmental Protection Agency 'Greenhouse Gas Emissions from Municipal Waste Management' September 1998 ES-1. This is the final draft which was modified to take on board a number of contested arguments by proponents of incineration: even so the greenhouse gas savings from recycling exceeded those from 'energy from waste' incineration by a factor of four.

[14] D.Gielen and T.Kram, 'The MATTER project on integrated energy/materials strategies for Western Europe', Paper to the ETSAP

workshop, May 1998, Berlin.

[15] USEPA 1998 op.cit.

[16] The model was developed by the Canadian consultancy firm REIC on the basis of waste composition and recycling studies in the UK. The results are reported in R. Murray, 'Creating Wealth from Waste', Demos 1999, p.39.

[17] The link between reducing and recycling waste and global warming has still to be recognised between (and even within) ministries in the UK. The DETR White Paper 'Climate Change: the UK Programme', published in November 2000 contained only three brief references to waste and gave it only marginal importance in the overall Strategy (pp 38, 81 and 184). The same Department's 'Waste Strategy 2000' treats the overall climate change impact as contingent on the specific circumstances of material and place, and suggests (on the basis of a report by the incineration-associated consultancy AEA Technology) that the new Strategy and the impact of the Landfill Directive will have only a marginal impact on carbon emissions (a reduction of 0.1-0.4 million tonnes). See Department of Environment, Transport and the Regions, 'Waste Strategy 2000', HMSO, Vol. 1 p.18.

[18] R.Lal 'Soil conservation and restoration to sequester carbon and mitigate the greenhouse effect', III International Congress, European Society for Soil Conservation, Valencia 2000.

[19] E.Favoino, 'Composting: a backbone of intensive recycling schemes' in: Ecologika, 'The Potential for a Recycling and Composting Led Strategy in Greater Manchester', Technical Papers, Greater Manchester Waste Disposal Authority, December 2001, p.5.

[20] D.J.Gielen, 'The MARKAL systems engineering model for waste management', paper prepared for the workshop 'Systems engineering model for waste management' Gotteborg, 1998.

[21] The arguments on the environmental benefits of recycling as against incineration, in particular with respect to plastics and paper, are more fully discussed in the London recycling plan prepared by Ecologika for the London Planning Advisory Committee and the Environment Agency, 'Re-Inventing Waste: Towards a London Waste Strategy', London 1998, Chapter 4.

[22] P.Hawken, A.B.Lovins, L.H.Lovins, Natural Capitalism, 1999, p. 3.

[23] European Environment Agency, 'Environmental Signals 2000', Copenhagen 2000, p.102.

[24] This is the argument of much

footprint research, which calculates the ecological footprint of contemporary modes of production. One example of this work, which looks inter alia at waste in the UK, is a study of the Isle of Wight funded by the waste company Biffa, which showed that the per capita footprint of the islanders was 2.4 times the size of the island, marginally less than the 2.5 ratio for the UK as a whole. See Best Foot Forward and Imperial College, 'Island State: an ecological footprint analysis of the Isle of Wight', Biffaward, 2000.

[25] A.Adriannse, S.Bringezu, A.Hammond, Y.Moriguchi, E.Rodenburg, D.Rogich and H.Schultz, 'Resource Flows: the Material Basis of Industrial Economies', World Resources Institute, Wuppertal Institute, Netherlands Ministry of Housing, Spatial Planning and the Environment, National Institute for Environmental Studies, Tsukuba, Japan, April 1997.

[26] Performance and Innovation Unit, Cabinet Office, 'Resource Productivity: Making More with Less', November 2001.

[27] For accessible versions of the argument see E.von Weizsacker, A.B.Lovins and L.H.Lovins, Factor Four, Earthscan 1997, P.Hawken, A.B.Lovins, L.H.Lovins, Natural Capitalism, op.cit.

[28] G.Gardner and P.Sampat, 'Mind over Matter: Recasting the Role of Materials in Our Lives', World Watch paper 144, December 1998, p.26.

[29] D.Gielen, T.Kram and H.Brezet, 'Integrated Energy and Materials Scenarios for Greenhouse Gas Emission Mitigation', paper for the IEA/DOE/EPA workshop, 'Technologies to Reduce GHG Emissions: engineering-economic analyses of conserved energy and carbon', Washington, May 1999.

[30] On the expression of social identity through things, including the old and the new, see the work of Pierre Bourdieu, and in particular his remarkable book Distinction: a Social Critique of the Judgement of Taste, Routledge, 1984.

[31] This definition came from the Commission's 1992 Report. It is quoted in J.Thornton, 'Pandora's Poison: Chlorine, Health and a New Environmental Strategy', MIT, 2000, pp. 347-8.

[32] Many examples of clean production initiatives are contained in the Journal of Cleaner Production, Elsevier Science. See also Thornton op.cit. Chapter 9.

[33] See E.Favoino, 'Trends in the Treatment of Organic Waste in Europe', in: Ecologika, 'The Potential for a Recycling and Composting Led Strategy in Greater Manchester', part

1, Greater Manchester Waste Disposal Authority, December 2001.

[34] These points echo a number made by two Cranfield design engineers, Chris Sherwin and Tracy Bhamra, in their paper 'Beyond Engineering: Ecodesign as a proactive approach to product innovation' in 'The Proceedings of Ecodesign 99: First International Symposium on Environmentally Conscious Design and Inverse Manufacturing', Tokyo, February 1999, pp 41-6. Their concern was with the product-centred, incremental use to which LCA has been put, rather than its use for designing new products and systems.

[35] M.Braungart and W.McDonough, 'Design for Reincarnation', Resource, April 2000. See also their article 'The Next Industrial Revolution' in Atlantic Monthly, October 1998.

[36] Op.cit.

[37] For North American and UK evidence see R.Murray, 'Creating Wealth from Waste', op.cit. Chapters 4 and 5.

[38] There are reports of some US recycling programmes being cut back for these reasons, losing their momentum, their political support and in the end their budgets. See Institute for Local Self Reliance, 'Wasting and Recycling in the United States', 2000, Grass Roots Recycling Network, Athens GA, 2000.

[39] Flexible specialisation is a term coined by C.Sable and M.Piore in their book, The Second Industrial Divide, Basic Books 1984, which was one of the first to recognise the character of the new paradigm. The new paradigm has also been referred to as Just-in-Time Production, Post-Fordism and Flexible Manufacturing. See also a key early work on the subject, M.Best, The New Competition, Polity 1990.

[40] Two of the most successful recyclers have been the Salvation Army and Oxfam – though neither has yet ventured into multi-material kerbside collection. The 250 members of the Community Recycling Network together are the largest kerbside recycler in the UK.

[41] One example arose when it was discovered that the Audit Commission and the DETR, under pressure from industry, had classified the reuse of toxic incinerator ash for construction as recycling, with the result that the best way of meeting the government's recycling targets would have been to incinerate all combustible waste in order to maximise the residual ash. This ignores (as do many other definitional disputes) the issue of the quality of recyclate discussed earlier.

[42] This is recognised in the EU working document on a future Bio

Waste Directive, where separate biowaste collections are proposed for all towns and cities with more than 100,000 population within three years of the Directive coming into force, and all towns and villages with more than 2,000 inhabitants within five years. The collections should be planned for household waste, as well as for biowaste from restaurants, hotels, canteens, schools, public buildings, shops, markets, food businesses and shops. See: European Commission, Working Document, 'Biological Treatment of Biowaste', 2nd draft, Brussels February 12th 2001.

[43] One of the UK's leading recyclers, the community enterprise ECT, uses acorn group marketing data, gathered by postcode, to estimate the composition and quantity of waste from any particular locality – on the basis of which it plans its rounds, forecasts its quantities of captured recyclables and estimates performance.

[44] The UK system of collection and disposal credits provided for such transfers between separated authorities, although collection savings have often been difficult to capture because of the lack of flexibility in contracts. In 1999/2000 Disposal Authorities paid an average of £23.87 for avoided disposal on 1.1 million tonnes of recycled or composted material, but only £0.92 for avoided collection on 32,000 tonnes diverted.

[45] G.Gardner and P.Sampat, 'Mind Over Matter: Recasting the Role of Materials in Our Lives', Worldwatch Paper 144, December 1998, p.15.

[46] L.D.Simone and F.Popoff, 'Eco Efficiency', MIT, 1997, p.3. The authors were at the time Chairman of the Minnesota Mining and Manufacturing Co. and of the Dow Chemical Company respectively, and chaired the WBCSD working group on eco-efficiency. See also N.Nemerow, Zero Pollution for Industry, John Wiley, 1995.

[47] For examples of waste reduction see L.D.Simone and F.Popoff op. cit., and the United Nations University Zeri Project for example of zero emissions.

[48] The problems of extending 'environmental management systems' (EMS) to product design and development is discussed by G.Ries, R.Winkler and R.Zust in 'Barriers to successful integration of environmental aspects in product design', in: 'EcoDesign '99. Proceedings of the First International Symposium on Environmentally Conscious Design and Inverse Manufacturing', Tokyo February 1999 pp 527-532. The discussion relates to experience in Switzerland. Although they highlight the difficulties, it is clear from their paper that the push for effective integration between EMS and product design is

strong, and that increasing numbers of firms are internalising environmental issues in their research and development (60% of 250 firms surveyed were integrating in this way in 1997/8, up from 20% two years earlier).

[49] For a remarkable analysis of the chlorine industry from this perspective, see J.Thornton, 'Pandora's Poison', op. cit. MIT 2000.

[50] See W.R.Stahel, 'The service economy: wealth without resource consumption?', Philosophical Transactions A, Royal Society, London 355, (June) pp 1,309-1,319. See also O.Giarini and W.R.Stahel, The Limits to Certainty, 2nd edition, Kluwer Academic Publishers, 1993.

[51] The auto project is one on which Michael Braungardt has been working as an exemplar of the new low resource economy.

[52] The Product Life Institute, 'The Shift from Manufacturing to a Service Economy 1998-2010', Geneva, p.165 (the report is available for US$/Euro 5,000 from the PFI, PO Box 3632, CH 12ll Geneva 3).

[53] See David Morris 'Building a new carbohydrate economy', Renewable Energy World, Vol 4 no 5, September-October 2001.

[54] Franklin Associates estimates that the new material 'Ecolean' has between 30% and 70% less environmental impact than the glass, laminated cardboard and aluminium it is designed to replace.

[55] Henry Ford made some trenchant observations in his autobiography on the old engineering order who dismissed his initiatives as unworkable, see My Life and Work, Heinemann, 1924.

[56] On the early development of the opposition to incineration in the US see B.Commoner, Making Peace with the Planet, Gollancz, 1990, Chapter 6.

[57] Sweden in 1990 relied on landfill and incineration in broadly equal proportions (44% and 41%) with recycling and composting accounting for 16%. In that year they amended their Solid Waste Act to set out the principles of Producer Responsibility and encourage dry recycling. Producer Responsibility legislation and subsequent ordinances were introduced in 1992-4, covering packaging, tyres and waste paper. By 1997 recycling and composting had reached 33% and they are presently in line to rise much higher when the ban on organics to landfills comes into force in 2005. In France, recycling was overshadowed by incineration until 1999, when the Environment Minister ordered the closure of 20 high polluting incinerators (with a further 40 on

probation) and ordered waste plans to be redrawn to given greater emphasis to recycling.

[58] The Dutch programme was in part a response to dioxin scares in the late 1980s, when high dioxin levels in cows' milk and dairy products were traced to incinerator emissions. It was found that none of the incinerators were complying with the required standards. After the rebuilding programme, there have been regular surveys which are still finding that not all the new generation of incinerators comply with the strict standards the Dutch have introduced.

[59] The Bio-Waste Directive was planned as a compliment to the Landfill Directive (for details see footnote 42 above).

[60] See the Commission's proposals for the sixth EC Environment Action Programme, published in February 2001 (ENDS Report 313, pp 46-48) and the speech to the European Waste Forum on June 21st 2001 by the Environment Commissioner Margot Wallström, which hinted at a possible shift away from product-based EC producer responsibility initiatives to a broader, materials-based policy.

[61] The Italian Decree no 22, which implemented a number of EU Directives, included a provision that all non-hazardous waste must be disposed in the region where it is produced.

[62] See Roger Crowe, 'Green finds a primary role in the boardroom', Financial Times April 12th 2001.

[63] The nuclear industry, for example, found itself beached in the 1970s as the result of concern about emissions, the disposal of nuclear waste and the cost of decommissioning. The phaseout of PCBs, CFCs and asbestos threatened firms dependent on these materials. Pesticide producers have found themselves attacked from four directions – the impact of pesticides (particularly those based on organochlorines) on workers in pesticide factories, on the farmers applying them, on water quality and on consumers of food with pesticide residues. In some instances the compensation claims for pollution incidents made on manufacturers (notably Union Carbide at its Indian Bhopal plant) have been so large that they have led to the rapid collapse of firms internationally.

[64] The pressure on major companies in the UK to incorporate environmental considerations into their decision making has been increased by the recent conclusions of the Turnbull Committee on corporate governance, which establishes guidelines for the management of environmental risk.

[65] R.Slater, 'State of Composting in the UK', Materials Recycling Handbook, Emap, 2001.

[66] John Gummer, for example, overrode the advice of his civil servants in allocating £12 million Capital Challenge funds to London boroughs because the Boroughs had produced detailed plans that promised a significant expansion of recycling in London. There are many similar examples from the period of office of Michael Meacher.

[67] Merrill Lynch, 'Pollution Control', September 1998 p.7

68 The system of recycling credits applied a parallel principle within the public sector, with provisions for arms length inter-authority transfers (according to disposal costs saved) that served as a price supplement.

[69] See the controversy surrounding the report by the Environment Agency Board member Paul Dalton on the inadequacy of the EA's regulatory practices on the ground, 'Just Who Does the Environment Agency Protect?', August 2001. A summary of the controversy appeared in an article by Paul Brown in the Guardian, September 12th 2001.

[70] John Turner in evidence to the House of Commons Select Committee on 'Delivering Sustainable Waste Management', op, cit. 'Minutes of Evidence' p.89.

[71] There are 15 compliance schemes, the largest of which, VALPAK, represents 3,000 of the obligated parties and accounts for 60% of the compliance 'market'.

[72] The Environment Agency estimates are contained in their nine regional strategies published in 2001. The results of the waste strategy model and a summary of the Landfill Directive RIA model results are contained in Annex B of 'A Way with Waste', DETR, 1999, Volume 2 pp 148-160.

[73] Manchester Waste Limited and the Manchester Waste Disposal Authority have been in dispute with the Environment Agency over the classification of the organic output from their mechanical treatment plants, which at the moment is classed as non-inert waste and subject to the landfill tax. See the House of Commons Select Committee Report, Environment, Transport and Regional Affairs Committee, 'Delivering Sustainable Waste Management, Minutes of Evidence', March 14th 2001, p.62.

[74] The collection authorities are bound to deliver their waste to such facilities under the terms of the Environmental Protection Act 1990 which gives disposal authorities first claim on any waste or recyclate in their area for which contractual provision has been made.

[75] PFI contracts have sought to introduce some sharing of these risks with the contractor, recognising that

this will lead to higher gate fees. A study for the DTI reported that gate fees in the initial PFI waste contracts, all of which were centred round incinerators, were 19%-26% above those of cost-plus contracts. See Impax Capital Corporation Ltd, 'The Influence of the PFI on Waste Management Pricing', Report for the New and Renewable Energy Programme, ETSU B/WM/00549/REP, 2000.

[76] That this conflict is a real one is shown not just by the low recycling rates of UK authorities served by incinerators but also by the recycling programmes in countries like Holland and Denmark which have had to fit in with the volumes and priority materials required by each country's stock of incinerators.

[77] There has been a recent shift in view in some parts of the waste industry. A recent document from Biffa commented that 'most in the industry agree that that at least 60% is a realistic target for diversion from landfill into biodegradation and recycling.' See Biffa, 'PFI Update', July 2001. Biffa has been an exception within the mainstream waste industry in re-assessing the role of waste management in the light of the need to re-establish biological and technical cycles.

[78] For a statement of this position see J.Rifkin, The Age of Access, Penguin 2000.

[79] The DTI consultation paper on renewable energy strategy emphasised EfW as a significant potential contributor to the renewables programme ('New and Renewable Energy for the 21st Century', DTI March 1999) and the 1999 Waste Consultation Paper took this up, concluding that 'the Government will continue to encourage the recovery of energy from waste, where this is the BPEO, as part of its renewable energy strategy.' 'A Way with Waste', DETR, 1999 vol 1, p.21. Nevertheless, in terms of climate change strategy, waste was given only marginal importance chiefly because the AEA report estimating the CO_2 savings from recycling omitted all energy saved from avoided virgin production (see footnote 13 above).

[80] 'Making Waste Work', DETR, 1995, p.53

There have also been controversies over toxic ash from the Sheffield plant and pollution in Dundee. In Sheffield tests of bottom ash showed dioxin levels at 150 ng/kg. In Dundee, a Friends of the Earth survey found high levels of contamination around the incinerator, which led to calls for medical screening of those living in the area. See Sunday Times, July 15th 2001.

[81] There were substantial delays in delivering WISARD, caused, it was said, because its designers had found it difficult to get it to produce results

supportive of the 'integrated option'. This was eventually solved, but after less than a year, the Scottish Environmental Protection Agency decided to end its compulsory use on the grounds that it always produced results favouring incineration.

[82] In the first half of the 1990s there was a small Supplementary Credit Approval programme to assist local authority recycling; and later individual awards were made under Capital Challenge and Single Regeneration Budget (SRB) programmes. The total was probably less than a tenth of the amount by which the UK remaining incinerators were subsidised.

[83] In a Parliamentary answer the Minister Michael Meacher said that this was not necessarily the case, but the Guidance continues to carry weight nonetheless.

[84] Op.cit p.58

[85] 'A Way with Waste', op.cit. vol 1 p.25 The wording was kept in 'Waste Strategy 2000', vol 2 p.77

[86] Op.cit. vol 2, p.19 'Waste Strategy 2000' in re-affirming this point said that EfW plants should be 'appropriately sized' and not crowd out recycling, but no geographical limits were set for the catchment areas so that EfW applications are being considered for areas where their capacity equals the whole MSW stream. See Vol 1, p.23 para 2.23.

[87] In September 2000, after Ministerial intervention, it was announced that priority in the allocation of PFI funds should be given to recycling, but the PFI terms and process still favour capital intensive projects and promote wholly inappropriate long-term contracts. As for the £140 million for recycling, none was earmarked for 2001/2.

[88] Proceedings of the Welsh Assembly, May 10th 2001, Cardiff.

[89] The data is for dry dustbin recyclables and is derived from DEFRA, Municipal Waste Management 1999/2000, July 2001, Tables 8 and 9, and from estimates made for UK waste composition by the Canadian waste analysts REIC. Target capture rates are from best practice programmes in the UK and Canada.

[90] The levels of organics found in residuals in the integrated food waste collection systems operated in Italy average 15%-20%. In the best schemes they fall to 10%. In Austria and Germany the levels average 40% and in the Netherlands 50%, partly because of the high diversion levels in dry recyclables in all these countries, and partly because of the widespread use of wheeled bins for residuals, which attracts a higher levels of organics than the Italian system (see inset 2).

[91] The Environment Agency issued a Consultation Paper 'Guidance on the Waste Treatment Requirements of Article 6(a) of the Landfill Directive' in late 2001. It defines 'treatment' narrowly, so that all residuals after source-separation for recycling would be considered as 'treated' in spite of the fact that their fermentability would be in no way reduced. This is another example of the UK's environmental minimalism, and is in line with British opposition to the EU's Bio Waste Directive.

[92] MBT has been largely ignored in the UK. Two plants are currently at the planning stage, but MBT has been scarcely considered in the waste plans of disposal authorities or the RTABs. Waste Strategy 2000 mentions MBT only briefly, noting its widespread use in Austria and Germany, and highlighting issues of pollution control found in some of the plants there. It is not included as an option in the models that informed Waste Strategy 2000, nor in the proposed 'integrated' option, in which incineration with energy recovery is put forward as playing 'a full and integrated part in local and regional solutions'. See Waste Strategy 2000, vol. 2, pp 78-85.

[93] A recent report by AEA Technology for the EU Commission 'Waste Management Options and Climate Change', ED 21158, 2001, estimated that MBT produced the lowest GHG flux (a negative flux of 340 kg CO2e/per tonne of MSW) of the various options for treating mixed waste prior to landfill. The principal reason is the sequestration of carbon through the landfilling of the stabilised organics following the MBT process.

[94] See Peter Jones of Biffa in his evidence to the Select Committee in October 2000, Environment, Transport and Regional Affairs Committee, Fifth Report, 'Delivering Sustainable Waste Management, Minutes of Evidence', March 2001 pp.7-8. There has been growing pressure from industry to increase the landfill tax in ranges from £25-£40 a tonne, but this is in part driven by the high cost of methods of residual treatment rather than the cost of recycling. The lower range estimate is based on the extra cost of moving to intensive recycling in all sectors of the economy, with the financing of recycling increasingly shifting to the market through producer responsibility legislation.

[95] In Italy three-stream systems have been introduced close to (or below) the costs of traditional collection. This has been in part due to the low cost methods of food waste collection and in part because of the scope for savings from the large number of regular collections (three or four per week in many Mediterranean countries) once food waste is separated out (see inset 2). An application of the Italian food waste model to Greater Manchester forecast that waste system costs would fall for

all nine boroughs. See M. Ricci, 'Guidelines and Costs for the Management of Food Waste in Greater Manchester' in Ecologika, 'The Potential for a Recycling and Composting-led Strategy for Greater Manchester', Greater Manchester Waste Development Authority, December 2001.

[96] The Essex High Diversion Programme, 'Prospectus', Chelmsford, June 2000. The local authority share of new fixed investment is estimated at £35.5 million. If this was publicly financed, it would lower the revenue support to £18 million, and require an overall sum of £53.5 million to fund the transition.

[97] The estimate does not include the recycling credits provided by Essex County Council (reflecting the costs of disposal and the landfill tax) nor of any increase in the costs of CA sites. Including recycling credits in funding requirements would add a further £3 million p.a., giving a total of £18 per household p.a.

[98] The transitional costs depend in part on the level of disposal costs. In a study for Greater Manchester similar to that undertaken for Essex, capital costs were £4.5 million and transition costs £25 million for a population 50% greater than that of Essex. The main reasons for the lower costs were the higher level of disposal costs (a saving of £36 for each tonne diverted from disposal was assumed for the nine Greater Manchester boroughs) and the use of the low-cost Italian food waste collection systems. By comparison, in Toronto, where disposal costs are high because of the need to export waste to landfills in Michigan, the Council recently announced its plans to achieve a 60% diversion target by 2006, with an incremental cost of only £5 a tonne.

[99] It might well be less in the event that a shift to four-stream systems would produce more packaging waste from the estimated 4.6 million tonnes in the domestic waste stream than the 1.2 million tonnes forecast as required for the 60% target. Supply would exceed demand and put downward pressure on PRN prices in the process.

[100] If the 50% target for the recovery of packaging waste in 2001 is met, it will have cost the 'obligated parties' some £100 million, little of which has gone to the municipal sector. The £100 million figure is given in the government's September 2001 consultation paper on 'Recovery and Recycling Targets for Packaging Waste'.

[101] The government is currently undertaking a five-year review of the performance of the Environment Agency. The draft report of this Review was summarised in ENDS no 320, September 2001. The report does not address the main issue that

has emerged in the conduct of the Environment Agency, which is the problem of getting a rule-based organisation to take a proactive role in environmental protection, coupled with the issue of regulatory capture.

[102] The New Opportunities Fund has developed fruitful methods of managing the bidding process, including joint seminars for applicants and individual specialist advice.

[103] The OECD has made waste minimisation, extended producer responsibility and changes in the mode of consumption the prime focus of its work on waste since 1994.

[104] Gielen, Kram and Brezet op.cit. (see footnote 29).

[105] USEPA, September 1998 op.cit (see footnote 13).

[106] G.A.Davis, 'Principles of Application of Extended Producer Responsibility' Proceedings of the OECD Joint Workshop on Extended Producer Responsibility and Waste Minimisation Policy, Paris March 2000, Part 1, pp.102-8. Gary Davis is from the Center for Clean Products and Clean Technologies, University of Tennessee.

[107] For other products and substances the EU has used bans – as in the case of the landfilling of tyres and the phasing out of CFCs in fridges and air conditioners, and of halons in fire protection systems.

[108] This was notably the case in the electric and electronic goods sector, where UK firms showed a marked reluctance to expand recycling in spite of the forthcoming EU Directive and the advances made in electronics recycling on the continent.

[109] Report of the Task Force of the Advisory Group on Packaging, DEFRA, November 2001.

[110] For a more detailed discussion see ECOTEC, 'Effects of Landfill Tax – Reduced Disposal of Inert Waste to Landfill', January 2000.

[111] See E.Darier (ed) Discourses of the Environment, Blackwell 1999, particularly the introduction by Darrier, and the chapter by T.W.Luke, 'Environmentality as Green Governmentality', pp 121-150.

[112] This is the position of Ulrich Beck in a succession of books on risk and modernity. Beck is a professor of sociology in Munich, one of the international centres of the re-insurance industry. See particularly his book Environmental Politics in an Age of Risk, Polity Press 1995.

[113] For a review of the problems surrounding scientific knowledge and its treatment within conventional risk assessment see M.O'Brien, Making Better Environmental Decisions, MIT

Press, 2000. The book also outlines a different approach termed 'alternative assessment'.

[114] A recent study that highlights the issue of information, hazards and governance is by the European Environment Agency, 'Late lessons from early warnings: the precautionary principle 1896-2000' which was published in January 2002. In light of the historical experience of hazards such as asbestos and BSE, the study considers how more accessible, science-based information and stakeholder governance in economic activity could minimise environmental harm and maximise innovation. The proposals have particular relevance to the issue of information and governance in relation to Zero Waste.

[115] Performance and Innovation Unit, Cabinet Office, 'Resource Productivity: Making More with Less', November 2001, op.cit.

[116] The former DETR has produced guidelines for business on reporting waste, which were aimed at helping companies measure the waste they produce, how waste management could be improved and achieve savings. These need to be extended to the materials productivity strategies outlined here.

[117] On alternative experiences of quasi-public institutions to provide technical support and advice to industry, see H.Rush et al, Technology Institutes: Strategies for Best Practice, International Thompson Business Press, 1996

[118] The Advisory Committee on Business and the Environment, 'Resource Productivity, Waste Minimisation and the Landfill Tax' August 2001. Another of its recommendations was to raise landfill costs and to use the extra tax revenues to fund resource productivity initiatives in the business sector.

[119] Lord Marshall, 'Economic Instruments and the Business Use of Energy', Treasury, November 1998.

[120] For a description of the programme see P.Hermens and T.van Roemburg, 'Dutch Perspective on Waste Prevention Target Setting', OECD Joint Workshop on Extended Producer Responsibility, op.cit. Part 2, pp 41-49, March 2000.

Proceedings of the OECD Joint Workshop on Extended Producer Responsibility and Waste Minimisation Policy, op.cit. March 2000, Part 1, Introductorary speech.

[121] On reuse and the ways in which consumers and local authorities can influence its expansion see N. and D. Goldbeck, Choose to Re-use, Ceres Press, New York, 1995.

[122] Proceedings of the OECD Joint Workshop on Extended Producer Responsibility op. cit.Part 1, Introductorary speech, March 2000.

[123] OECD, 'Environmental Strategy for the First Decade of the 21st Century', adopted by OECD Environment Ministers May 16th 2001, and the accompanying 'Environmental Outlook'.

[124] M.Braungart, 'Waste Must Equal Food' Green Punkt Scheme Annual Report 2000, 'Recycling as a Source of Raw Materials', p.78. He continues 'natural processes are not eco-efficient but rather eco-effective. Nature does not save, it "wastes" – however with suitable resources (just look at a cherry tree in spring – what a "waste" of energy and raw materials.)'

[125] J.Waller-Hunter, op.cit.

126 For a good recent summary of his ideas see W.R.Stahl, 'From Design for Environment to Designing Sustainable Solutions', in: UNESCO, Our Fragile World: Challenges and Opportunities for Sustainable Development, EOLSS Publishers, 2001, pp 1553-1568.

[127] A summary of the industrial metabolism approach, based on ex post material flows, is given in R.U.Ayres, 'Industrial metabolism: theory and policy' in: R.U.Ayres and U.E.Simonis (eds), Industrial Metabolism: Restructuring for Sustainable Development, United Nations University Press, 1994.

[128] On the shift in environmental policy from centralist regulation to market instruments and the issues arising see M.R.Chertow and D.Esty (eds), Thinking Ecologically: the next generation of environmental policy, Yale 1997.